my
LOVE

my
LIFE

D1707825

my LOVE
my LIFE

A *Devotional*
FOR ANY DAY

Betsey Kelley

TATE PUBLISHING & *Enterprises*

My Love, My Life: A Devotional for Any Day
Copyright © 2008 by Betsey Kelley. All rights reserved.

Scripture quotations marked "KJV" are taken from the Holy Bible, King James Version, Cambridge, 1769. Used by permission. All rights reserved. Scripture quotations marked "NLT" are taken from the Holy Bible, New Living Translation, Copyright © 1996. Used by permission of Tyndale House Publishers, Inc. All rights reserved.

The opinions expressed by the author are not necessarily those of Tate Publishing, LLC.

Published by Tate Publishing & Enterprises, LLC
127 E. Trade Center Terrace | Mustang, Oklahoma 73064 USA
1.888.361.9473 | www.tatepublishing.com

Tate Publishing is committed to excellence in the publishing industry. The company reflects the philosophy established by the founders, based on Psalm 68:11,
"The Lord gave the word and great was the company of those who published it."

Book design copyright © 2008 by Tate Publishing, LLC. All rights reserved.
Cover design by Kandi Evans
Interior design by Jonathan Lindsey

Published in the United States of America

ISBN: 978-1-60462-879-1
1. Christian Living: Practical Life: Personal Growth: Women   2. Religion: Devotional
08.02.19

Dedicated to my husband, my best friend; Brandon and Zach, our treasured gifts from God; and my parents who told me about Jesus.

Acknowledgements

I started this book twenty-three years ago, never really believing it would be finished much less published. God started this work early in my married life, but it wasn't until the last two months of 2006 and early 2007 was brought back out and completed. I did not have enough experience in the Lord or in my marriage to write this book that many years ago. However, time presented itself and the Lord has been such a positive reinforcement to keep me at it until completed.

To Ralph, my love, you are the consistent, loving man from who I draw great strength and admire with all my heart. Life has been complete with you by my side.

To our boys, Brandon and Zach, you are the treasure of our home. We are blessed with you as gifts from God. Thanks for your support in the writing of this book.

To Lorie, my niece, I could not have gotten "everything right" as far as editing my work without you. You took on this great responsibility and made my job easier by getting rid of "wordy sentences," stopping me from using the word "that" too often and taking care of all those misplaced commas! You were my constant cheerleader.

Many thanks to pastor, Dr. Billy R. Norris. You graciously gave your time and lent expertise in verifying the scriptures to make sure I did not take things out of context or misuse the Word. Every single time I sent back devotions for you to review, you always encouraged me to finish the book.

To my parents, this book will be a surprise. Mom and Dad, your faith has touched my life in the greatest way possible. I am blessed to have you as my parents, who love God with all your heart and raised me to do the same.

A million thanks to those at Tate Publishing for guiding me through this process. You took a great risk to work with an "unknown" in your business. I hope you will not be disappointed.

Finally, to God, my life ...I owe *everything*! You are the reason for the book in the first place. This book originated with You giving birth in my mind and the heart to write. I will forever be indebted to You for all Your goodness that follows me and my family.

Contents

Foreword

As I began this task of reading this material that Betsey has written, I recognized very quickly, "These are good." With anticipation I awaited the next glimpse into the happenings of this dear family.

I have read various devotional materials. This one is unique in the sense that the author opens up her life experiences in her marriage and her home and draws from those rich experiences. She challenges us to grow in our marriage and family relationship in often amusing and witty anecdotes. Then, she adds rich commentary and Scripture to help the reader draw nearer to our blessed God. Betsey's love and faith in her family and her Lord is "real." She doesn't just "say" the right things ... she "lives" the right way. Knowing this makes her annotations so helpful since they are written with complete integrity.

As you peruse each section, draw from the immense wealth that is available to you in these readings. Your marriage and family relationship will grow deeper and stronger. And the most important relationship with God our Father and His Son Jesus Christ will mature and develop and become ever so sweeter.

Dr. Billy R. Norris

Dr. Norris is Senior Pastor of the Winston-Salem Church of God of Prophecy. He received his Doctor of Ministry degree from Christian Life School of Theology (a subsidiary of Beacon University based out of Columbus, Georgia). He resides in Kernersville, North Carolina.

A Good Thing

Ralph, we have a "good thing" in our marriage. It is far from perfect and we have certainly had our ups and downs. But I can say our marriage has been more than I expected or dreamed it could be (for the most part). I will leave room for improvement.

We met in college. After the first date, I went back to the dorm and found a quiet place and told God that Ralph was special. I wasn't sure what God had planned for us, but I knew Ralph was different from all the others. Ralph made the decision from the first night not to date anybody else (and he didn't). Furthermore, he made the comment to his roommate that he just might "marry this girl" (meaning me ...oh yeah!). Must have been some first date, huh? Actually, we just went to a football game, but we were "meant to be." God saw us through a wonderful dating relationship that started in the month of August. In November, a year later, we said "I do" to each other. No regrets. *I would jump at the chance (as I did the first time) to say "yes" to you again, Ralph!*

I heard someone say their marriage was not anything they had anticipated or desired. I hear women speak of their marriage and many of them express they "would not do it over again" if they had the chance. You do what you have to do to make things "good" in this sacred union called marriage. Don't verbalize the thoughts of "regrets" in conversations with your friends. Begin to expect good things, satisfaction, rewards, and a great life with your companion for the rest of your days. Do I really believe there can be one man for one woman for all of their days? Yep, I do!

You got me, Babe. And, I am real glad … I have found a good thing (you have too).

The Bible says, "A friend loveth at all times …" (Proverbs 17:17, KJV). My partner is my best friend. We have some "struggles" in getting along *all* the time, but God's love and help is there at *all times*.

Don't write off your marriage! Marriage was instituted by God, and He certainly puts His blessings on those who seek His face concerning this sacred union. Prayerfully bring your marriage before God and allow Him to make it good. Parents, encourage your children to let God find that "helpmeet" for them. When God created the world, He saw that everything was "good." The only thing He mentioned that was not good was for man to be alone.

Then the Lord God said, "It is not good for the man to be alone. I will make a helper who is just right for him." So the Lord God caused the man to fall into a deep sleep. While the man slept, the Lord God took out one of the man's ribs and closed up the opening. Then the Lord God made a woman from the rib, and he brought her to the man.

Genesis 2:18, 21–22 (NLT)

But God made them male and female from the beginning of creation. This explains why a man leaves his father and mother and is joined to his wife, and the two are united into one. Since they are no longer two but one, let no one split apart what God has joined together.

Mark 10:6–9 (NLT)

Whoso findeth a wife findeth a good thing, and obtaineth favour of the Lord.

Proverbs 18:22 (KJV)

When I Come Back

I was engaged to be married to Mr. Wonderful! The only problem? It was going to be six long weeks until our wedding day before I would see him again. Ralph lived in Virginia, I in North Carolina …we were worlds apart. I cried so hard when he left for Virginia. I thought (and felt like) I was going to die.

Mr. Wonderful did something pretty wonderful as he left to go back to Virginia. He came by my workplace and left me a note stating that the next time he came to see me he would be taking me back with him for good, to be his wife, and he would never leave me alone for weeks at a time again.

I clung to those words like dryer sheets cling to fresh laundered clothes. He would be coming back …to get me and take me home with him! What a comfort. I practically ruined that note by carrying it around and rereading it so often those six weeks. I made it during his absence by knowing he was coming back and we would not have to be separated anymore.

Ralph sure looked good when I saw him at the end of those long six weeks. We were married and it really is great to be with the one I love!

I love living life here on this earth. Yet, I realize someday it will all come to an end. One day I will breathe my last breath, but that's okay. I enjoy living today. Still, there are times I long to be with the One who gave His life for me. I long to see Him face to face and desire greatly to spend eternity with Him. His name is Jesus. He left me a note (along with everyone else) in His Word telling me that He would come back someday to take me home to be with Him.

I believe in Heaven. I believe Jesus has prepared a place for you and me as His children. One day He will come to take us to that place He has prepared for us. Talk about something to look forward to!

Sometimes life is hard. We long for the comfort of home and to rest in our Heavenly Father's arms of love. Anticipating that and all the promises His coming and our home going affords brings great delight to the child of God.

And to think we will never be separated from Him again! Being *like* Him, *with* Him, *forever*! I do yearn for that time … and it's sooner than most of us realize.

> In my Father's house are many mansions: if it were not so, I would have told you. I go to prepare a place for you. And if I go and prepare a place for you, I will come again, and receive you unto myself; that where I am, there ye may be also.
>
> John 14:2, 3 (KJV)

> And if our hope in Christ is only for this life, we are more to be pitied than anyone in the world.
>
> I Corinthians 15:19 (NLT)

> Looking for that blessed hope, and the glorious appearing of the great God and our Savior Jesus Christ.
>
> Titus 2:13 (KJV)

Unspeakable Gift

Ralph has given me wonderful gifts over the years. Yet, the one gift that tops them all is his undying commitment to me and our family. Sounds a little dramatic, huh? Material things are great. I am not against receiving anything Ralph wants to buy me (hint, hint), but I would not trade what Ralph has given me through commitment in our marriage for all the money in the world.

Commitment, loyalty, safety, trust ...wow! This is what women are looking for in marriage. Undying commitment is how I describe Ralph's loyalty to me. It does not fade when the going gets rough. He doesn't change his mind when he gets tired or weary with the day in, day out responsibilities. He doesn't give up in the face of just trying something different.

It is Ralph's constant and consistent resolve to this marriage that proves he loves me. Because the flowers, candy, or other gifts that may have come frequently during the first years of our marriage do not happen as often, that does not in any way cause me to feel less loved. Every time he walks out the door to his job, proves he loves our family by being the best provider he can be. Being there to support us in whatever we are involved in proves he loves us. Taking responsibility as "head" of our home (his right) in leadership and living with honor is strength to our family. He does not shirk from his duties of husband, father, provider, and Christian example, but does all with remarkable strength.

I am not boasting. I am only focusing in this book on Ralph's strengths as a man, husband, father, and Christian. I choose to focus on his strengths instead of his weaknesses. I do admire my husband. He returns this admiration by being my unspeakable gift ...the treasure of my heart.

Ralph, I am wealthy in a lot of ways that have nothing to do with money, and it is because of you in my life!

God gave His unspeakable gift to us. This gift cannot be compared to *anything* in this world! His unspeakable gift is His only Son Jesus. Unspeakable—meaning words cannot explain, definition cannot be given to accurately describe this Gift.

Jesus' commitment is never shaken. Bad days do not alter this commitment. Mistakes do not alter this commitment. Being fickle does not alter the commitment from Jesus. His commitment sticks day in and day out.

His Gift—His Son—when accepted into your life becomes the Gift of all gifts! Nothing will ever top or come near the value of this Gift. It is indescribable. Do you get what I mean? We have no words that represent how wonderful and magnificent this Gift is. A great price was paid for this Gift. Jesus dying on a cross for you is proof of God's love. Do not take lightly the price paid. No amount of money or good deeds can buy this Gift. Accept Jesus in your life and give thanks daily to the Giver of this Gift.

Thanks be unto God for his unspeakable gift.

II Corinthians 9:15 (KJV)

For by grace are ye saved through faith; and that not of yourselves: it is the gift of God.

Ephesians 2:8 (KJV)

For God so loved the world, that he gave his only begotten Son, that whosoever believeth in him should not perish, but have everlasting life.

John 3:16 (KJV)

And anyone who believes in God's Son has eternal life...

John 3:36 (NLT)

Once and For All

We have all heard that something worth doing is worth doing right. Ralph is a firm believer in this. If we have heard him say, "touch something one time," we have heard him say it close to a thousand times (at least). He has reminded the boys and me that whatever we do, do it well, do it right, touch it one time. Touch it one time means complete it so it never has be finished by someone else or redone, otherwise you are wasting your time (and probably someone else's). It is so easy to get in a hurry and half-heartedly do something or leave it unfinished because of lack of interest or lack of time. Ralph lives what he preaches about this at home and on his job. The boys have received many pep talks when a chore or project was left undone. Some things take time in getting accomplished and we just have to settle down and do it ... do it right ... do it well ... touch it one time. Am

I repeating myself? I guess this is okay because Ralph repeats it over and over to us all the time!

Jesus is the master at doing things well, complete, and right. He desired to make us His own and died on a cross that we might be saved. He gave Himself *once and for all* as a sacrifice for our sins. He did this *once* and it never has to be done again. It was complete, perfect and right.

Don't think this wasn't a tremendous sacrifice. He even asked His Father if it was His will to let "this pass." However, He knew God's love for us was bigger than what His Father was asking Him to do. Jesus became willing to do what He was asked. He loved us perfectly and completely. He was willing to lay down His life for us.

He will never have to die for our sins again. He became the perfect sacrifice and "*it was finished.*" Am I repeating myself again? That's okay. His Word tells us over and over of His love and describes in detail how He suffered for us ...to make us His own!

> Father, if you are willing, please take this cup of suffering away from me. Yet I want your will to be done, not mine.

> Luke 22:42 (NLT)

For in that he died, he died unto sin once ...

Romans 6:30 (KJV)

For Christ also hath once suffered for sins ...

I Peter 3:18 (KJV)

...It is finished. Then he bowed his head and released his spirit.

John 19:30 (NLT)

A Merry Heart

Ralph has a sense of humor (dry though it may be), and is witty. Our family loves to laugh. I have a hanging on the wall over our kitchen table that reads *Live Well, Love Much, Laugh Often.* Humor can dispel dreadful emotions, smooth over fierce arguments, and lighten a serious moment. Any parent knows what it is like to be frustrated when their kids act up in public. One incident stands out more than any other in our children's lives which bears telling.

We had a new baby and our other son was three years old. We went out to eat and as soon as our food was delivered to us, the baby started crying. Almost immediately, our three-year-old son turned his milk over and completely soaked himself. He started crying (rather loudly). My husband took him to the bathroom to get him dried off and comfort him while I took care of our crying infant.

When my husband returned from the restroom, an elderly gentleman seated near us stated, "It gets better." We just smiled, packed everybody up, left our food on the table and walked out the door with both boys crying. Just as my husband reached for the handle, our three-year-old met the car door with an impressive thump. *Wham!* The car door hit him in the head. (For your information, he was okay ...not even a bruise or bump appeared.)

Strangely enough, Ralph and I started to laugh at the same moment! I know ...this is awful when both kids are crying and one's clothes are totally soaked with milk. To top it off, the poor little fellow gets his head slammed by the car door. What were we thinking? I don't know what came over us, but the laughter completely released our tension. We got over it, went home and took care of the kids.

Humor ...it's necessary to see the lighter side, funny side, ridiculous side (sometimes) in matters to survive and keep a sound mind.

Thanks, Ralph, for all the laughs. Sometimes when we argue, a grin creeps up on your face and then the laughter explodes. Of course, at the time I don't see anything funny. But the funny thing is I've learned you are not laughing at me but with me. (You are laughing with me, right?) Yeah, it's very good to laugh … a lot!

I am a firm believer that Jesus has a sense of humor. I believe He loves to hear our laughter, and enjoys smiles and expressions of happiness. If He did not believe in laughter, then I would be in trouble!

The Lord tells us in His Word to rejoice many times over and be glad. I will do this. He has certainly taught me that it is more than okay to have fun in worship, going to church and in serving others.

A glad heart makes a happy face …

Proverbs 15:13 (NLT)

A merry heart doeth good like a medicine …

Proverbs 17:22 (KJV)

… happy is that people, whose God is the LORD.

Psalms 144:15 (KJV)

Always be full of joy in the Lord. I say it again—rejoice!

Philippians 4:4 (NLT)

That Look

Ralph has that "look" that lets you know when he is displeased. Ask our boys. The "look" that says you've crossed the line, your joke went too far, you disobeyed...you know, the "you're-in-trouble" look.

We laugh about this "look" when everything is all right in our family, but it is not funny when you receive it. This expression can make you feel quite bad. I have also been a recipient of this "look." I have my own "look," but I don't think it is quite as scary!

There is something about "getting caught" doing wrong. You are troubled when you disappoint a person you respect. Especially, when you have been warned and know better but do wrong anyway. Many times, Ralph has only had to display the "look" and it was all that was needed to get his point across with our boys.

I wonder if our sons will take on that "look" with their kids someday. They know how to do it so well and we laugh when they imitate their father. *Ralph, I think you got that look from your father and it just may very well be passed down to our boys. We will see.*

Ralph, I'm glad for the "look." Following the "look" usually come consequences for the wrong done ... and isn't that usually what keeps us from doing that again?

Our heavenly Father loves us so much. He is merciful and kind and such a wonderful Father to us. However, there are those times when we deliberately do things that are just not right and He has to correct us. Correction can be difficult to take, especially when we are forewarned not to do something and turn around and do it anyway.

One such example was Peter in the Bible. Jesus forewarned Peter that he would deny knowing Him, not one time but three times! Peter just knew he couldn't do such a thing and brushed off the warning. However, he did do just that ... deny knowing Christ three different times in a short period.

The Bible says the Lord *looked* upon Peter. Oh no, "that look!" Can you imagine how Peter felt—so bad, in shock, sad—that he had disappointed the One who loved him so. And he had been warned. However, Jesus' look was one of knowing this would happen, disappointment, sadness, compassion, and love all wrapped up in one expression.

Our disobedience may result in the "look" from the Lord from time to time. He is merciful and will forgive. He never stops loving us! However, we must continue to do what's right and expect the "look" when we do wrong. He is a loving Father who corrects His children.

> But Jesus said, "Peter, let me tell you something. Before the rooster crows tomorrow morning, you will deny three times that you even know me."

> Luke 22:34 (NLT)

> At that moment the Lord turned and looked at Peter. Then Peter remembered that the Lord had said, "Before the rooster crows tomorrow morning, you will deny three times that you even know me." And Peter left the courtyard, weeping bitterly.

> Luke 22:61, 62 (NLT)

God remembers our frame (makeup) and takes that into

consideration and, therefore, His love and forgiveness is ours!

For he remembered that they were but flesh ...

Psalm 78:39 (KJV)

Prepares a Place

For the last six years, Ralph has put forth great effort in finding a place for us to celebrate our anniversary. It has been fantastic getting away for the weekend, just the two of us!

Around October, Ralph starts researching bed and breakfast inns and cabins to find that right get-away spot for us. He has done a very good job in selecting the places where we have stayed.

November 2006, marked our 25th anniversary! I decided to try my hand at finding a place for us and did a *little* research, but settled on something rather quickly. I informed Ralph of my "pick." He looked it over and wasn't quite sure it was the place, but because I had my mind settled on that particular one then he agreed.

The place was nice. It was a bed and breakfast inn. It was more for families than couples. There was very little privacy. The room we occupied was between two other rooms where children's lofts were added. We arrived before the other "couples/families" did and found out we were to share a "common room and a kitchen" with all the others. There was a large deck in the back overlooking a small pond and it was lovely, but we also shared that with the other two "families" next door. Breakfast the next morning was served in a solarium which was very nice, but we had no idea we would be sitting with fourteen other people! Romantic, huh? Anyway, we had a good time.

I think I will put finding a place back on your shoulders, Ralph. You have done an excellent job in picking the right spots for us. You put forth more effort in researching and asking more questions about the places than I obviously did. I'm already looking forward to next year's get-away, and with great pleasure wait for you to make all the preparations!

God wants to spend time with us. He has given us nice homes and places to visit here on earth that brings great pleasure. However, there is a place prepared for you and me when this life is over. It is prepared by God! He has taken special care to make it "more than what we could ever imagine."

We will go to this special place prepared for us someday. We will not be disappointed ... it will be "just right." You might want to start preparing and make sure you are ready to go when the time comes. "Your room is ready ..."

Let not your heart be troubled: ye believe in God, believe also in me. In my Father's house are many mansions: if it were not so, I would have told you. I go to prepare a place for you. And if I go and prepare a place for you, I will come again, and receive you unto myself; that where I am, there ye may be also.

John 14:1–4 (KJV)

And the foundations of the wall of the city were garnished with all manner of precious stones ...

Revelation 21:19 (KJV)

...and the street of the city was pure gold, as it were transparent glass.

Revelation 21:21 (KJV)

And God shall wipe away all tears from their eyes; and there shall be no more death, neither sorrow, nor crying, neither shall there be any more pain: for the former things are passed away.

Revelation 21:4 (KJV)

Children Are a Gift

After being married for four years it hit me. I wanted to have a baby! I wanted the two of us to become a "family." So did Ralph. At twenty-eight years old, I became a mom ...the happiest day of my life. That happiest day was repeated again three years later when the second baby arrived!

Our children are the joy of our lives! They are very different in nature and we have thoroughly enjoyed the ride of parenthood. Now, don't get me wrong, there have been some days and there have been *some days*!

Brandon is in his third year of college and Zach is a senior in high school. Our days of having these guys around are few in number. We have taken these gifts from God and done our best. We are not quite through and Ralph is injecting into every conversation some important detail of life that they just might need. *(He can ask a lot of questions, can't he, guys?)*

Brandon has a great smile, plays the guitar and sings, is very witty and smart, athletic, has great discipline, and is much like his dad (hey, that's not sooo bad). Zach is very funny, creative, athletic, plays the drums and guitar (a little), sings, is spontaneous, intelligent, and is much like his mom *(you are blessed, son)*. They both have something going on in their makeup from both of us, yet they have become their own persons and we like what we see. We are very proud of these guys!

We don't know what they will actually "be" when they grow up (we are still trying to figure that one out for ourselves), but one decision they both made at a young age was to accept Jesus Christ into their lives.

The guys are in a contemporary Christian band. Brandon writes most of the songs, plays guitar, and sings. Zach sings and plays drums (also learning on the guitar). *In His Name* was started a little over a year ago. We ask God to take them as far as He will in this ministry. We support them all the way.

We have had very few times of crisis with these guys …only a couple stand out. Because of great communication with the guys and God's help we got through these. Our love is still present even when wrong is done (I am still finding out things Brandon did "in the past" that I didn't know about ...thanks to Zach!). We will soon experience the "empty nest" syndrome, but we are "peacock proud" of our young men. *It has been our extreme pleasure to be your mom and dad.*

Children are a gift from God. Cherish this gift (or gifts) and take excellent care with what God has given. Family is important to God. The greatest treasure in our homes is our children, and having God in our homes to guide us in raising them is a necessity.

We need God's help in raising our children. His help is there for us through His Word and by wisdom that only He can give us when sought after.

God loved His Son. He found pleasure in Jesus. He asked a hard thing of His only Son. However, Jesus loved us as much as His Father and did what was asked of Him. God asked His Son to die on a cross so we could become His children. See the smile of God as He takes great pleasure in His Own (you and me). His love is ever present even when we (His children) "mess up." That is a good thing to know.

Children are a gift from the Lord; they are a reward from him. Children born to a young man are like arrows in a warrior's hands. How joyful is the man whose quiver is full of them!

Psalm 127:3–5 (NLT)

...we are the children of God.

Romans 8:16 (KJV)

And since we are his children, we are his heirs. In fact, together with Christ we are heirs of God's glory ...

Romans 8:17 (NLT)

...for he that toucheth you toucheth the apple of his eye.

Zechariah 2:8 (KJV)

I like the way the NLT version interprets "apple of the eye" as "my most precious possession."

I Know

Several years ago, Ralph was out of work for seven months. We thought this crisis would never end. He worked odd jobs with very little pay. However, we did get through this and a job offer was made (thank God!).

Ralph has already been where I am now. My home business and work is coming in very sporadically and may be ending in the near future. Ralph knows. He truly understands what I am feeling. He can acknowledge my pain, worry, and fear.

I talk to people and try to explain what I am going through. They look at me and say they know, they understand. I know good and well they have never gone through this situation and, furthermore, have no earthly idea what I am dealing with! I look at them with a pleasant expression on my face but on the inside where nobody sees but God, I am rolling my eyes up in my head! *Forgive me, Lord!*

You can be sympathetic to a person who is in a tough situation without saying you understand what they are going through. You cannot relate to their hurt and pain without having experienced it yourself. If you say you know and understand without having gone through a similar situation, it may add salt to the wound.

I hope I was there for Ralph when he was out of work for so long, but I did not understand like I do now. He has been there for me the last four months and his comfort is genuine. Ralph draws from the comfort He received at God's hand when out of work and is now able to comfort me going through the same thing.

I know you know, Ralph. Thanks for being there. Just knowing that you know has helped.

We face things that other people have experienced. Sometimes it still doesn't help, even when they know! But when God lends His ear to listen to our cry for help …that is a different matter.

Maybe you doubt that God "up there" can relate to you being "down here." However, He tells us that because of

His being here on earth for a period of time, He can feel for us and relate to what we face. We have His attention. He does for us what nobody else can do because He does know (in more ways than one).

So then, since we have a great High Priest who has entered heaven, Jesus the Son of God, let us hold firmly to what we believe. This High Priest of ours understands our weaknesses, for he faced all of the same testings we do, yet he did not sin.

Hebrews 4:14, 15 (NLT)

Even though Jesus was God's Son, he learned obedience from the things he suffered.

Hebrews 5:8 (NLT)

Like as a father pitieth his children, so the Lord pitieth them that fear him. For he knoweth our frame; he remembereth that we are dust.

Psalm 103:13, 14 (KJV)

He comforts us in all our troubles so that we can comfort

others. When they are troubled, we will be able to give them the same comfort God has given us.

2 Corinthians 1:4 (NLT)

My Hiding Place

Husbands should provide their wives with a "hiding place." That entails not only a physical environment but also a place where you feel safe with your partner in your relationship. A "place" where your needs are met and you are loved and respected. It is where you run to when things do not go so well "out there."

Ralph provides a hiding place that lets me know he is proud to have me by his side. I am not talking about being a "trophy wife," but I am speaking of being loved, cherished, and kept deeply in mind each day. Ralph provides strong arms that know how to embrace at just the right moment.

I do not like being away from Ralph very long. I do not like to travel very far from home. This is because our marriage and home do not represent a place to get away from or a place of tension or stress for me. It is a place of refuge, safety, laughter, love, and most of the time, pleasant experiences.

Thanks Ralph for being my hiding place by opening your arms of love when I am overwhelmed by "stuff." Here I come...

God is my hiding place. He offers me rest and safety from "out there." I can run to this place anytime and will be made welcomed and taken care of.

There is nothing weak about running to God when we are scared, tired, or perplexed. He is our present help in trouble. I can take courage and be strengthened by this "hiding place in God." You must try it out when you find yourself with no other place to run. He will receive you and not cast you aside.

Run to this "hiding place!" Don't wait one more day, one more minute or one more troubled moment. The Word of God makes it very clear how to get to this place, hear it:

Then shall ye call upon me, and ye shall go and pray unto me, and I will hearken unto you. And ye shall seek me, and find me, when ye shall search for me with all your heart.

Jeremiah 29:12, 13 (KJV)

Thou art my hiding place; thou shalt preserve me from trouble ...I will instruct thee and teach thee in the way which thou shalt go; I will guide thee with mine eye.

Psalm 32:7, 8 (KJV)

The Lord is my rock, my fortress, and my savior; my God is my rock, in whom I find protection. He is my shield, the power that saves me, and my place of safety.

Psalm 18:2 (NLT)

...hide me under the shadow of thy wings.

Psalm 17:8 (KJV)

I Am In Your Corner

Everyone needs somebody in their corner cheering them on from time to time. We need that cheerleader in our lives that will "root" for us when we need that extra support in what we are doing.

Ralph is an encourager for our boys in whatever they do. At the ballgames, Ralph is heard! The guys can expect the "box out," "step into it," "run," "get the ball," or whatever needs to be said in a particular sport. I watch the boys steal a glance over at their dad to see if he is watching, or if he has a helpful "sign" to give them. Ralph makes sure he attends just about every activity they are involved with. He is there. That means more to the guys than anything that could be said. Of course, it is *icing on the cake* when they meet up with their dad after the occasion and he says, "Good job."

We let the boys know we are there for them when they have a difficult problem to face. They know they can talk to us about anything. They know they have our support in whatever they do. Sometimes, we are not enthusiastic about a choice they make, but hopefully we do a pretty good job of letting them know we support them in their decision.

Ralph has lent his support to me all our married lives. I can always count on him to be there in my corner when I need that extra boost of "wishing me well." Ralph has certainly backed me up in writing this book. He is a team player as I direct the choir, minister to the youth and married couples, and he supports my home business and other "stuff" going on in my life. And yes, he has given in many times (against his better judgment) when I wanted to play a certain instrument, and of course, never quite followed through. Recently, I informed him I wanted to play the violin and he just laughed and shook his head (now does that sound like encouragement to you?) and said, "Whatever." I think I sort of blew my chance on that one when I rehearsed how I would probably sound (*screech!*) while learning to play the violin.

Anyway, thanks, Ralph, for "whatever it is" we decide to do you are pretty much game. You are there to pick us up whenever things don't quite work out the way we hope. You are also there with a beautiful smile on your face with pride when we do accomplish something!

God is our "cheerleader." He is for us, lends support, and is quite pleased when we accomplish our goals. It is through Him we can do all things.

He is on your side! He loves to see His children do well and prosper. Go find your support in Him the next time you are having marital problems, a job promotion comes up, considering a career change, going back to school, and the list can go on. He is your Heavenly Father *in your corner* with a big smile cheering you on!

Keep Him first in all you do. Pray about every decision. And when you have His blessing ...*go for it!* He knows you can do it!

Encourage one another in the Lord. At times, we need *God in skin* (people) to embrace, give us a pep talk and encourage us when we feel down or need that extra "push" to have the courage to do what is before us.

> Beloved, I wish above all things that thou mayest prosper and be in health, even as thy soul prospereth.

> 3 John 2:2 (KJV)

The Lord is on my side ...

Psalm 118:6 (KJV)

Be strong and of a good courage ...

Joshua 1:6 (KJV)

This is my command—be strong and courageous! Do not be afraid or discouraged. For the Lord your God is with you wherever you go.

Joshua 1:9 (NLT)

For I the Lord thy God will hold thy right hand, saying unto thee, Fear not; I will help thee.

Isaiah 41:13 (KJV)

I can do all things through Christ which strengtheneth me.

Philippians 4:13 (KJV)

Don't Let the Sun Go Down

It is very hard to argue with someone when they will not argue back. That's Ralph, or was, until he spent the last twenty-five years with me. I think I wore him down a little. Early in our marriage, I would become upset and angry about things and would let Ralph know. More times than not, he would listen, nod his head and say, "Okay." *Okay … what? Is that all you have to say, Ralph?*

We had only been married for about six months when I misjudged something that I *thought* I saw. I approached Ralph with this and decided I wanted to go "home," and I meant "home, home." Ralph very quietly spoke and said, "Okay, I will put you on the plane tomorrow morning and you can go home." Where was the argument? I was ready for "*words*" and I got nothing but this reply. It took all the fire out of me. I sheepishly replied, "That's all right … I don't want to go home … I'm sorry … I didn't mean it," and so on and so on.

I used to be a turn-to-the-wall woman when the argument lasted into the nighttime hours … you know, the silent treatment type. I would lie in bed and "stew" over the situation. It was not long before I would hear (let me get the dictionary so you know what I am talking about) "breathing with a rough, hoarse noise while sleeping." Yes, snoring! Here we are in the "middle of a crisis" and Ralph is sleeping like a baby! Does he care? Does he understand how important this is? Obviously not!

Over the years, this petty stuff gets worked out very fast and I fall asleep right along with Ralph. Besides, we cherish a good night's sleep. I am quite *historical* but less *hysterical* than I used to be. I do not play the "silent game" anymore. *(Come to think of it ... Ralph, did you enjoy the "silent times?")*

Ralph, it is not worth being at each other's throat over matters that most of the time we can't remember anyway. Your not arguing early on in our marriage took a lot of fire out of me and I have valued your calm spirit. Let's continue to make sure whatever is bothering us is worked out before the day ends (zzzzzzzzz). Ralph?

Uncontrolled anger is very dangerous in a marriage. Being upset robs our peace of mind, wastes precious time, and can make you sick physically. We all get frustrated and angry. However, name calling, verbal abuse, and physical abuse should never enter the picture in a couple's relationship where God is the center of the marriage.

God helps us deal with anger. If you are having problems with anger issues in your marriage, towards others or even with your children, seek God for help. Allow Him to teach you how to be quiet and use words that will calm the situation instead of "setting it on fire."

Being angry and bitter can bring "death" to a relationship, and can certainly play a role in physical illness. We can learn from God's example how to forgive and get along with others. When anger controls us then we sin ...that's biblical (really!).

> And don't sin by letting anger control you. Don't let the sun go down while you are still angry, for anger gives a foothold to the devil.
>
> Ephesians 4:26, 27 (NLT)

> Don't use foul or abusive language ...Get rid of all bitterness, rage, anger, harsh words, and slander, as well as all types of evil behavior. Instead, be kind to each other, tenderhearted, forgiving one another, just as God through Christ has forgiven you.

Ephesians 4:29, 30 (NLT)

A soft answer turneth away wrath: but grievous words stirs up anger.

Proverbs 15:1 (KJV)

Do all that you can to live in peace with everyone.

Romans 12:18 (NLT)

What's the Plan?

Whenever I or the boys approach Ralph with a new idea, new business proposition, purchasing some item that really is expensive, etc., he always asks the question (*in unison, boys!*), "What's the plan?" If we present a new idea or desire to get "something" that costs lots of money, he expects us to have at *least* come up with a plan to make it happen.

It just bursts my bubble when he questions me about the plan! I am usually so excited about the *idea* and he can't get beyond the *plan* not being formulated. So frustrating! And yet, he is right. You think we would know by now that we should spend time on executing a plan to go along with the idea. Maybe the reason we don't come up with a plan is because we half-way expect him to do that part.

Ideas, dreams, and goals won't occur unless they come off paper, and effort is made to see them come to fruition. There are those people who have the greatest ideas and desires "in their head" but cannot come up with ways to see them accomplished.

We cannot be afraid to try, to start and to work at it. Ralph lives this and whatever confronts him he tackles it head-on. I gain strength and courage watching him and our boys take on projects, activities and job promotions with determination. There is nothing wrong in seeking the help of those who have already accomplished what we hope to. That's a very wise thing to do. We can gain great wisdom and know-how from those who have already "been there and done that."

All right, Ralph, the next time I talk to you about doing something "new," I will try to spend as much time on planning this new project, as well as sharing my hopes for this to come to pass.

Many times in our churches we experience a "lull" or "rut" in our services and growth, and we become "criticizers." Instead of coming up with a plan to see growth, we complain of what's not being done. A leader doesn't mind a little constructive criticism as long as it is followed up with suggestions or a plan to improve things.

We must sit down and "count the cost" of a project before running head-on without knowing what it will require of us. We should ask ourselves questions such as, "Am I willing to spend the time, cost, and effort to see this through? Is my plan a good one? Can this work? Will I need the help of others to accomplish my goal?"

Failing to plan is planning to fail. If something is worth pursuing and doing then it is certainly worth sitting down and planning your strategy to make it happen. I believe (and the Word even tells us) that the Lord expects us to take into account what we will need to do in order to see "things achieved" in our lives. Seek Him to understand what your next step is.

> But don't begin until you count the cost. For who would begin construction of a building without first calculating the cost to see if there is enough money to finish it?

> Luke 14:28 (NLT)

> Or what king, going to make war against another king, sitteth not down first, and consulteth whether he be able with ten thousand to meet with him that cometh against him with twenty thousand?

> Luke 14:31 (KJV)

A wise man will hear, and will increase learning; and a man of understanding shall attain unto wise counsels.

Proverbs 1:5 (KJV)

Hear counsel, and receive instruction, that thou mayest be wise in thy latter end.

Proverbs 19:20 (KJV)

Whiner

Murmuring and complaining got so bad in our household a few years back, we decided to see if we could go without whining for a week. If we complained, we were to pay up—a dime for every time we opened our mouths to find fault about something. We had quite a few dimes in the jar by the end of the week. I was the loser (worst complainer) and Ralph the winner (whined the least). The boys fell somewhere between us in the "little game." We learned a lot about ourselves. I wonder if we had continued on with that "game" and implemented the behavior of being less critical, how much better individuals we would be today.

"You ole whiner," Ralph shouted out to our youngest son, Zach, one day. Boy, did it make Zach angry. I laughed! It *was* funny! (I have a bad habit of laughing when I should not do so.) I do not remember what Zach was complaining about, but this little phrase has helped him (and all of us) with not whining as much anymore.

"You ole whiner" has become a favorite saying around our house.

Nobody likes to be around someone who complains all the time. You just don't want to hear it. It has a way of bringing you down in your thoughts and emotions. Many parents give in to the whining of their children because it is absolutely draining.

I have caught myself "whining" and came to realize it got on *my* nerves. How much more was it grating on my family and those around me who heard it? In observing Ralph, I have to hand it to him—he does remarkably well with not complaining about things. He just does whenever, however, whatever, without bringing it to everyone's attention. Ralph's mother exhibits this "whine-less nature" and he learned well from her example.

Oh well, I gotta do better. Woe is me! How about you? Have you gotten in your *whining* today?

The Lord is more tolerant of His children than we are many times of one another. But I do wonder if He grows somewhat weary of our complaining.

He tells us in His Word that we are to do *everything* without arguing or whining. Is this possible? I mean,

His Word says this ... not me. The scripture to bear this out will follow, but this weighs heavy on my mind and heart as I write this. *This is possible*, for His Word commands us to do this. Wow! I am going to have to pray about this in my life. How about you? I have something to work on and it is *doable* in the Lord! Are you in this with me?

> Do everything without complaining and arguing, so that no one can criticize you ...
>
> Philippians 2:14, 15 (NLT)

> Neither murmur ye ...
>
> I Corinthians 10:10 (KJV)

> And *when* the people complained, it displeased the Lord...
>
> Numbers 11:1 (KJV)

Indulge Thyself

Ralph and I had only been married a few months. He, like any other young married man or woman, relished the idea of being his own person—no one to tell him what to do, when or where to go, or how late he could stay out. He was his own man ... free to do as he pleased. He sat one day eating an ice cream bar. He decided on another and then another. I merely questioned as to how many ice cream bars he planned on eating. Good-naturedly, of course, the spiel followed of his being his own person and doing as he pleased. You know, "I'm no longer a child. I can eat as many of these as I like. In fact, I just may eat the whole box of ice cream bars if I so choose!"

I don't remember Ralph eating the *entire* box of ice cream bars, but I do remember him feeling a little puny after devouring most of them. He soon realized it was not so great after all to "do whatever, whenever, however" just because he could. Yes, he clearly paid for it and even commented on how sometimes you really do need that "stern, guiding hand" whether it be from Mom or from me ...his wife (new mom—*not*!).

Freedom is practiced by every man, woman, boy, and girl. However, it cannot be abused without consequence. Indulging without restrictions, boundaries, guidelines, or common sense can lead to less-than-desired outcomes.

God's Word gives us a lot of room to be us. Yet, there are restrictions and boundaries that we must abide by or we actually begin to experience ill effects in more ways than one.

I am very glad that I have the hand of God (through His Word) to guide me and give me direction. I find there is nothing weak or binding about adhering to the Word and being obedient to Him as He "orders our steps" for the day, every day.

Spiritual liberty starts when we ask God to:

Order my steps in thy word ...

Psalm 119:133 (KJV)

and then Divine support lends the hand needed for us to see that:

The steps of a good man are ordered by the Lord: he delighteth in his way.

Psalm 37:23 (KJV)

They rejected my advice and paid no attention when I corrected them. Therefore, they must eat the bitter fruit of living their own way, choking on their own schemes.

Proverbs 1:30, 31 (NLT)

Walking With Wise Men

We are affected by the people we associate with. There are those people who inspire you, make you laugh and leave you feeling alive and refreshed. And then there are those who absolutely suck every ounce of energy out of you by the time you have spent just ten minutes with them in a telephone conversation. You know, the "so-called friends" who are so negative, unhappy, nothing ever goes right in their life. Those are the people I am trying to spend less time with since I don't seem to make any difference in turning them around to enjoying life and seeing the good.

I *had* a friend that would call every single day ...sometimes more than once a day. By the time I would hang up from that conversation, I was feeling down, depressed, and fatigued ...anything "not good" could be added to the list. I never traced my depressed feeling and anguish to this caller until I started discussing it with Ralph. It was an eye-opener for me to realize this "friend" was killing me emotionally, and setting me up to be depressed the rest of the day. *Thanks, Ralph, for helping me see that this was directly coming from my friend.* Ralph encouraged me to let the answering machine kick in or do whatever necessary for a few days to create distance between us. I did just that and, *whew,* did I feel better. The calls became less and less frequent as I took charge and decided I was not going to get caught up in this less-than-desired relationship.

You become whatever you surround yourself with. If people are fun, caring, loving, wise, and joyful then that's what you will be. If you are around those who are negative, mean-spirited, cynical, and depressing then you will soon take on that demeanor and act the same way.

Ralph has tried to impress on our sons to choose the right friends. He has also expressed how they should be good friends to others. The guys have been told over and over that they need to be very careful who they associate with, and should trouble arise, they are to understand they could be just as guilty by association.

Ralph doesn't give anyone much time if he sees they are not going to "enhance" the relationship. We both are trying to be a "good friend" to those we spend time with. It makes you feel good to have someone tell you they enjoy being in your company. *I especially enjoy being in your company, Ralph!*

The Bible makes it very clear that those we associate with affect us greatly, and cautions us about spending time with the wrong people. There are those in our families, church and communities that have so much wisdom and kindness to offer. We should seek out these people to befriend. It would be beneficial for us to "sit at their feet" and learn from them.

There are very special people in my life, and I do call them friends as they have added to my life a great friendship, a listening ear and can be counted on in good times and bad. If you cannot positively influence someone who is "draining you dry," by all means remove yourself from this relationship. Pray for that person to allow God to make the difference in them.

We become more like God when we spend time with Him—more loving, special, kind, giving, patient, and the other things that He is. We begin to take on His characteristics and "act as He does." People will see this when they spend time in our presence. Make sure they take away "good things" when they leave a conversation or visit with you. Let God's goodness in you rub off on others!

He that walketh with wise men shall be wise: but a companion of fools shall be destroyed.

Proverbs 13:20 (KJV)

Whoso keepeth the law is a wise son: but he that is a companion of riotous men shameth his father.

Proverbs 28:7 (KJV)

Don't do as the wicked do, and don't follow the path of evildoers. Don't even think about it; don't go that way. Turn away and keep moving.

Proverbs 4:14, 15 (NLT)

Go from the presence of a foolish man, when thou perceivest not in him the lips of knowledge.

Proverbs 14:7 (KJV)

Yet we hear that some of you are living idle lives, refusing to work, and meddling in other people's business. We command such people and urge them in the name of the Lord Jesus to settle down and work to earn their own living. As for the rest of you, dear brothers and sisters, never get tired of doing good. Take note of those who refuse to obey what we say in this letter. Stay away from them so they will be ashamed. Don't think of them as enemies, but warn them as you would a brother or sister.

2 Thessalonians 3:11–15 (NLT)

...be thou an example of the believers, in word, in conversation, in charity, in spirit, in faith, in purity.

I Timothy 4:12 (KJV)

Therefore all things whatsoever ye would that men should do to you, do ye even so to them ...

Matthew 7:12 (KJV)

Self-Worth

I have had a home business for eleven years now and have enjoyed every minute of it (just about). Unfortunately, my work has dwindled over the past four months and I am about to see it go "under." I have been saddened and am not quite sure why this has happened. Hopefully, everything will turn out okay. However, I have gone through the last four months feeling a loss of self-worth.

Ralph has been there and is doing the best he can with support, love, and encouraging words. I refuse to be comforted by his kind words because I don't believe them anymore. He tells me I am a great wife, mom, youth leader and choir director. He supports me in all the roles I play in our family and church community.

Nothing is helping me in this area of feeling "worthless." For some reason, I feel my self-worth is tied up in my business and the paycheck I bring home. It feels good making a contribution financially to my family. It is nice feeling there is a part of me aside from being a wife, mom, church member, and leader. This is my "little world" and I am proud of it. I took a correspondence course after the kids started school and earned a certificate in my business and felt good about it. Now, how am I supposed to feel when that is quickly fading?

The Lord has begun a work in me. He is opening my eyes to see that my self-worth is not who I am, the business I run, the amount of money I bring home or tied up in our house or cars. My self-worth is found in Him— God Almighty! I am made in His image and it is "whose I am" that makes all the difference. It has taken me a while to embrace this but today I have! I am important to God. All the roles I play in this life come after my "role of being His daughter." I will be okay because I believe Jesus is the Son of God—and that is power in my life! I believe He has started a new purpose for my life.

Ralph, as of today, I will not only hear your words of validating who I am but will believe them and live them in honor! Thank you for being patient during this four-month period of "scraping the barrel" in my business and never giving up on me. I love you!

You are cherished and loved. The Word says this better than I can about self-worth:

I will praise thee; for I am fearfully and wonderfully made: marvelous are thy works; and *that* my soul knoweth right well.

Psalm 139:14 (KJV)

For God so loved the world, that he gave his only begotten Son, that whosoever believeth in him should not perish, but have everlasting life.

John 3:16 (KJV)

We love him, because he first loved us.

I John 4:19 (KJV)

The Lord will work out his plan for my life ...

Psalm 138:8 (NLT)

Not that we are sufficient of ourselves to think anything as of ourselves; but our sufficiency is of God.

2 Corinthians 3:5 (KJV)

For we are God's masterpiece. He has created us anew in Christ Jesus, so we can do the good things he planned for us long ago.

Ephesians 2:10 (NLT)

…and he was called the Friend of God … *[So are we!]*

James 2:23 (KJV)

Casting all your care upon him; for he careth for you.

2 Peter 5:7 (KJV)

Who is he that overcometh the world, but he that believeth that Jesus is the Son of God?

I John 5:5 (KJV)

Think On Me

If you want to get closer to your spouse that you feel distant towards, think about them, reflect on your relationship, and then make time for them.

I think back to the story of a wife and husband whose relationship had grown cold towards each other. The wife observed their daughter skipping around Dad, hanging around Dad, helping Dad and going wherever Dad went. Her husband just doted on this little daughter of his. The wife almost envied the relationship and closeness that her daughter had with her daddy. The wife realized if she wanted to become the one her husband doted on as well, she should take lessons from her daughter and "spend time" with her husband, go wherever he went—whether she wanted to or not—and just treasure being with him. It did not take long for the "spark" to ignite in their relationship as the couple spent time with each other.

In writing this book about my love (Ralph) and my life (God), I have found myself drawing closer in both relationships, simply because I have deliberately "thought" on them. I have allowed time to reflect on why I love them and how they have affected my life in such a wonderful way.

Ralph has written me many love letters through the years. He wrote many letters during our dating months. I feel cherished because he thinks about me so much. At one point while we were dating, Ralph became very busy with starting a career. I was used to hearing from him daily by phone or receiving letters or cards several days out of the week. For *nine whole days*, I didn't hear anything from him or receive any mail. I was livid and scared! Pretty soon, I started doubting whether he truly loved me. Since we had stayed in such close contact, this totally devastated me. I began entertaining thoughts of doubt and fear that his love had faded. I continued sending cards. He was never in to receive my phone calls. Finally, his "busy time" passed and he let me know he was sorry and still loved me, that nothing had changed. What a relief!

We can get busy in our lives and spend our time on everything and everybody else but our companions. This is detrimental to the relationship.

Ralph, you have taught me that simply "thinking" about you and/or us brings back those "little butterfly" feelings in my stomach again! I really appreciate the calls I get from you every day from your work stating you are just calling to see how I am and how my day is going. Thanks for thinking of me. In fact, these days if you do not call me by mid morning, what do I say in my phone call to you? "Are you too busy to talk to your wife?" Can't you just hear me saying that?

God thinks on us! How about that? He takes the time to think about us and He is a busy God. Remind yourself through His Word that he has thoughts about you.

My thinking on God and who He is and what He does for me keeps me close to Him. I can tell when I am not as close to Him. It is always because I have stopped reflecting often on Him and His Word. Failing to talk to Him soon follows. Of course, that doesn't last long. When you love someone you begin to miss them! I begin to miss what the Lord and I have. Sweet communion each day and His presence are lost when time with Him and keeping Him in my thoughts begin to wane.

Take joy in knowing we are on God's mind:

> How precious also are thy thoughts unto me, O God! how great is the sum of them! If I should count them, they are more in number than the sand: when I awake, I am still with thee.

Psalm 139:17, 18 (KJV)

> For I know the thoughts that I think toward you, saith the Lord, thoughts of peace, and not of evil, to give you an expected end.

Jeremiah 29:11 (KJV)

> But I am poor and needy; yet the Lord thinketh upon me; thou art my help and my deliverer; make no tarrying, O my God.

Psalm 40:17 (KJV)

I Am Your Help

Ralph is intelligent and capable of doing multiple tasks at one time. However, all this seems to escape this man when he has to find something at home. Just the simple task of finding an article of clothing can become too difficult for this otherwise competent person.

Ralph's bedroom closet is pretty neat and tidy. One shouldn't have a problem trying to find anything. However, when he can't find something, he informs me so that I will go and look for him. It amazes me that what he is looking for is right there staring at him. He might have to move an article of clothing one way or the other just *slightly* for it to be found, but there it is! I think he just stands in front of the closet and if it is not visible to his eyes then he declares it can't be found. *Glad I can help, Ralph.*

If one of the boys gets hurt and it is just me with them, I can handle things okay. If Ralph is home and present for the crisis on hand, then for some reason I give myself permission to "fall apart" and you'd think I was totally inept as a mom. I don't know what comes over me. I suppose I feel a little like Ralph standing in front of his closet—just let someone else take care of it. *Glad for your help, Ralph!*

I am very glad for a companion who is there to help when I need him. Ralph will be there for me if at all possible every time. Sometimes though, it is just not possible ...

When our oldest son had his first car accident, Ralph was out of town. I felt my stomach fall to the floor when I received the phone call. My youngest son and I went to the accident scene. I called Ralph, and of course, he felt terrible about not being there. He was leaving right away but it would be several hours before he could get to us. I called several people and no one was available to come. I felt very alone but only for a short while because my *real help* showed up ... God! Glad for your help, Lord!

I don't know what I would have done without God the night of our son's accident. Everything was okay. The car was totaled but our son was all right and that was all that mattered. He walked away shaken, but physically fine.

There are those times when *nobody* can be there for you. Get this: *Every time* God is there for you! When you experience a time when nobody can be there, I encourage you to call on God for He will show up.

God *is* your present help when trouble arises. You can prove Him over and over in this matter. Many times He will make a way of escape and other times He will walk you through the storm. Either way, you can depend on His help.

I have called upon thee, for thou wilt hear me, O God ...

Psalm 17:6 (KJV)

I sought the Lord, and he heard me, and delivered me from all my fears.

Psalm 34:4 (KJV)

God is our refuge and strength, a very present help in trouble.

Psalm 46:1 (KJV)

My help cometh from the Lord, which made heaven and earth.

Psalm 121:2 (KJV)

Our help is in the name of the Lord ...

Psalm 124:8 (KJV)

For I hold you by your right hand—I, the Lord your God. And I say to you, "Don't be afraid, I am here to help you."

Isaiah 41:13 (NLT)

This Is the Way

We have moved twelve different times in our twenty-five years of marriage due to Ralph's career in retail. Those twelve times happened in just nine of those years! I got quite good at packing up, so if you need somebody to help you pack, I am your person.

Pennsylvania, that foreign country (may as well be to this Tar Heel gal), was our home for a while. As I spent time with the Lord in prayer, He began working on my heart that we were going to relocate. I shared this with Ralph and he stated that he had heard nothing from work about relocating. I continued to seek God and it was revealed that we were moving to New York! I once again shared this with Ralph and he just let me know that this couldn't be, as he had not been informed of anything on this matter from his work. I was so sure of what God had showed me that I started packing! I took down our curtains, packed up dishes and started getting rid of "stuff" that needed to be thrown away. Ralph didn't know what to think. We had only been married for two years. He suddenly had this wife who is packing up the house with no *earthly indication* that we were moving! However, two weeks later he was informed that we were moving to Buffalo, New York. I was way ahead of the moving game ... we had to be there in two weeks. New York, here we come. It was the right thing to do.

There was a time when Ralph was offered a position in another town of the same state we lived in with the company he worked for. He was told he would receive a call in just *one hour* and needed his decision on the position. With Ralph working, he did not have the time to seek the Lord in this very important matter. I told him to give me most of the hour to talk to God and then call me back. (After the above situation, Ralph didn't question what I got from God anymore.) I sought the Lord and discussed the matter with Ralph for a few minutes; we felt it was "okay" to make this move, and we did. It was the right thing to do.

Several years down the road (after the children had come along), Ralph was given an option to relocate to another town in the state in which we lived. We were very concerned about moving the boys again and wanted to make the right decision. We called on God! One day while in the basement of our home, I got a clear message from the Lord on what we were to do. I knew without any doubt we were to move ...again. While searching His Word I "happened upon" (if you want to believe that) a particular scripture, but I really believe I was led to it by God. This scripture simply said, "This is the way, walk ye in it." I shared it with Ralph and we stepped out on His Word that this was what we were supposed to do. We moved again. It was the right thing to do.

We have settled down the last fifteen years and are enjoying where we live. Thank God! However, we will always be open to relocating if God so chooses ...I think! *(Just teasing, Ralph, you know that).*

There are times when we find ourselves in the "valley of decision" and need direction in what to do. I believe God can let us know what the best course is to take. If I do not hear directly from Him in a matter then I have found He is okay with either way we decide.

Take your time to make a decision if you have time on your side. I believe if a decision has to be made in a short period of time, God is ready to give us His perspective on things. Just be ready to accept what He thinks is best, it might be different than what you had in mind. His will for us in some of our moves was not what I would have chosen, but I would rather do what is best (and that is His desire—the best for me) than to take matters in my own hands and really mess things up (oh yeah ... I've done that too).

How do you hear God's voice? By looking into His Word and sometimes it is a "knowing" in your mind and heart. You may hear God speak to you about a matter through a message or while talking with a good friend. I have listened to preaching and teaching of men/women of God. They did not know my situation, but God knew and led them to instruct me without them even knowing I was receiving an answer to prayer.

This is the way, walk ye in it.

Isaiah 30:21 (KJV)

My voice shalt thou hear in the morning, O Lord; in the morning will I direct my prayer unto thee, and will look up.

Psalm 5:3 (KJV)

The Lord hath heard my supplication; the Lord will receive my prayer.

Psalm 6:9 (KJV)

I will hear what God the Lord will speak ...

Psalm 85:8 (KJV)

I will answer them before they even call to me. While they are still talking about their needs, I will go ahead and answer their prayers!

Isaiah 65:24 (NLT)

Honor Mom and Dad

My parents moved four miles from us about two and a half years ago. They had just moved in their new home for only two weeks when my mom became very ill. Dad called our house about 2:00 a.m. on a Monday. Without hesitation, Ralph and I got in the car with our sons and headed to their house.

That night started a whole new way of life for my parents and our families. Mom had four ulcers and, in the process of finding this, was diagnosed with heart problems. Triple bypass surgery followed just a few days later. Mom suffered a stroke by the time she returned home. She was also diagnosed with Alzheimer's. My dad has done an amazing job in taking care of her.

Ralph was by my side through the many hospital stays, ER visits, and helping out in their home. He took off work several times and headed back a little later to make up for lost time. Ralph watches over me and cares for me during this very upsetting period in our lives. We may be in this process for a while and it is comforting to know he is there for me as well. *Let me say this again, Ralph, thanks!*

Ralph has honored my parents and been there for them like he would have his own. I appreciate the time he spends with them and doing things to help out. He respects the lives they live and truly loves them. Someday this will come back to him whenever he needs care and special attention.

Our parents do so much for us. This is not truly recognized until we are older and have children of our own. I feel we have a responsibility to help take care of our parents as they grow older, especially when medical problems arise and assistance is needed. Decisions about this care are often difficult to make. Husbands and wives need the support of each other in these times.

I encourage you to honor your parents all their lives. Enjoy time with them. Eventually, their minds and bodies will deteriorate and you will need to carve out some time to do whatever is necessary to help them.

In the Word, the command of honoring your parents comes with a promise! Read on to find this out.

Honour thy father and mother; which is the first commandment with promise; That it may be well with thee, and thou mayest live long on the earth.

Ephesians 6:2 (KJV)

Take care of any widow who has no one else to care for her. But if she has children or grandchildren, their first responsibility is to show godliness at home and repay their parents by taking care of them. This is something that pleases God.

I Timothy 5:3, 4 (NLT)

Rules

We have rules to abide by in our household. The boys have kept most of them and challenged us on others. I like one definition of rules that Webster gives: "the usual way of doing something."

Since our oldest son has been in college for three years, it is out of respect for his father and I that he abides by the rules already set in our home when he returns for visits. He has no curfew now, but out of courtesy to us he comes in at a decent hour at night so as not to disturb us (we appreciate that).

Both boys let us know where they are going, how long they expect to be out, and who they are going with. They know Ralph is going to ask anyway, so they go ahead and volunteer the information. Thanks, guys!

Ralph sets guidelines for our boys and consequences follow when those are not adhered to. The boys may think we are too hard on them (especially their father, I tend to give in too often), but as they have gotten older they appreciate these guidelines and tell us so (imagine that!).

I heard a young lady speak of the boys' curfew and guidelines. She is not required to follow any rules in her household, and certainly does not have a curfew. I will never forget the look on her face and what I heard in her voice when she told me she wished she had parents who cared about her. She understands the guidelines set for our children are because we care about them and their safety. Not having rules to abide by may seem great for a short while, but everyone needs those parameters and boundaries set for them.

Ralph, you are consistent in those guidelines for the boys. I am a little "wishy-washy" in these matters but am glad for your "stick ability." You know when to extend curfews and change the rules as the boys mature. I believe the respect the boys have for us keep them from challenging us too often in this area of our lives. We have a lot to be thankful for ... good guys who abide by the rules.

God has rules laid out for us in His Word. He wants

us to embrace them. These rules are given because God cares for us. Living by His rules assures a better life. He wants what is best for His children (as we do for our children). Therefore, His commandments are set forth for our good.

Just as our children pay for not abiding by guidelines in our homes, we will suffer when by choice we do not abide by God's rules. We express thankfulness to our children when they do what is expected of them. God is very pleased when we live the Word. His Word is there to keep us safe. He loves us that much.

> But don't just listen to God's word. You must do what it says. Otherwise, you are only fooling yourselves.

> James 1:22 (NLT)

> If ye keep my commandments, ye shall abide in my love ...

> John 15:10 (KJV)

> But the love of the Lord remains forever with those who fear him. His salvation extends to the children's children

of those who are faithful to his covenant, of those who obey his commandments!

Psalm 103:17, 18 (NLT)

If ye love me, keep my commandments.

John 14:15 (KJV)

Jesus answered and said unto him, If a man love me, he will keep my words: and my Father will love him, and we will come unto him, and make our abode with him.

John 14:23 (KJV)

Those who obey God's commandments remain in fellowship with him, and he with them ...

I John 3:24 (NLT)

Keep Singing

I love to hear Ralph sing. Our boys love to *watch* their dad sing. Ralph has a good singing voice (which I like to hear). He also sings with his whole heart (and body), which the boys like to "imitate." He can be funny to watch. *Zach, you have to show us how your dad sings. You do this so well.*

I know Ralph. He feels what he sings to the Lord. Ralph truly "makes a joyful noise" when he sings. His face expresses this joy and he is not afraid to show it.

He can sing quite loud, and I look over in church often and inform him that he is heard above everybody. *What do I usually say, Ralph? "Calm down!"* He just smiles and continues on singing "from his heart." It is real for him. He is giving this expression of praise and joy to the Lord because he is motivated by His God to do so.

There are times when Ralph's heart is heavy, but a song still comes from his lips because He knows the giver of life! Through singing, Ralph works his way to victory in difficult moments.

Ralph, honey, you just keep on singing as loud as you want to. You are blessing others and God, we realize that. Albeit, you are funny sometimes when you sing, but I mean this in the most "adoring way" so take it as given.

Now whether Ralph sings love songs to me, well, that is another story ...

We are to make a joyful noise unto the Lord. Music and song are excellent ways to express joyful praise to God. Good Christian music can soothe a worried heart and mind. The next time you find yourself a little stressed, go for it, sing with all your heart a praise to God. See what this does for you. It will lift your spirit!

Worship in song and music is a very important part of church services. It unites people as they lift their voices together to magnify God. In many church services, the worship music helps us to forget about everything "out there" and focus our minds on God. I see hearts moved by music and the message in songs as often as I see souls blessed by the Word of God. It is a powerful tool to use in worship to our Lord.

Sing unto him a new song; play skillfully with a loud noise.

Psalm 33:3 (KJV)

But each day the Lord pours his unfailing love upon me, and through each night I sing his songs, praying to God who gives me life.

Psalm 42:8 (NLT)

Sing praises to God, sing praises; sing praises unto our King, sing praises.

Psalm 47:6 (KJV)

And whenever the tormenting spirit from God troubled Saul, David would play the harp. Then Saul would feel better, and the tormenting spirit would go away.

I Samuel 16:23 (NLT)

singing psalms and hymns and spiritual songs among yourselves, and making music to the Lord in your hearts.

Ephesians 5:19 (NLT)

Read the book of Psalms in the Bible every chance you get. This is a book of 150 spiritual songs and poems. This hymn-book is wonderful to meditate on.

Maps, Instructions, Directions
... Who Needs Them?

Relocation from one state or city to another has been a big part of our lives as Ralph's employment has required us to do so. We have lived in a couple of big cities, Buffalo, New York, and Philadelphia, Pennsylvania. Finding my way around these cities proved to be too complicated for me. But then, I don't like maps, reading instructions, or directions. I am your basic "see-what-I-can-do-on-my own" type person.

Now, Ralph is quite different, in that he buys every map available, sits and studies the map (for what seems like forever), and carefully draws little circles on the map in order to help us better reach our destination. He has tried with *great effort* to get me to understand the necessity of maps, asking questions and following those instructions to avoid "going in circles." However, I am still pretty lousy when it comes to reading maps (ask him ... never mind!).

Ralph tries to help me follow instructions when I try to assemble a craft or put together an object. I just dive right in without knowing if I have all the parts or what to do with those parts. I have ruined a few projects in my time because I did not want to take a moment to read the instructions. It is too complicated to mess with all that stuff. Then I give it to Ralph for him to salvage. I wonder if that's why he always says, "Honey, if you'll just wait 'til I get home, I'll be glad to help you with that, okay?"

God's Word is our road map to heaven. How often have you and I discarded His Word like we would a map all because we feel as if we are losing precious time to sit and read, let alone study instructions that we may not fully understand. Is the Bible just too complicated so we ignore it altogether?

Confusion about the Christian life can many times be cleared up just by taking the time to read the Word. This must be done by seeking direction from God, and allowing Him to teach us His laws. That is part of the work of the Holy Spirit in our lives—to teach us.

There are "seasoned saints" (those that have followed God for many years) all around us who have taken much time to study the Word. Seek out those people you know who have an active daily prayer life and Bible study. I am sure they would be glad to impart knowledge that the Lord has given them through the Word. As you grow in reading and studying this road map to heaven, you will learn more of its instructions and directions and will be able to implement them in your daily life. It gets easier, especially when the Holy Spirit is sought in our understanding of the Word.

> Thy word is a lamp unto my feet, and a light unto my path.

> Psalm 119:105 (KJV)

> Take fast hold of instruction; let her not go: keep her, for she is thy life.

> Proverbs 4:13 (KJV)

Get all the advice and instruction you can, so you will be wise the rest of your life.

Proverbs 19:20 (NLT)

None Like You

I have "the best" husband in the whole world! That's the way you should feel about your spouse (and probably do). I can't imagine life without Ralph. I can't imagine life with anybody else (and don't imagine it). My eyes are for Ralph only.

Ralph is not perfect and neither am I. We are okay with that and make exceptions for our weaknesses and draw upon our strengths. When you realize you have the best partner in the world, you have just honored your marriage and companion in the greatest way possible. It is called "respect."

It is very good and satisfying when you are loved for who you are. If Ralph was always trying to change me then we would have a problem. This is something I do not experience with him, as he accepts me for being me. That is refreshing.

When you come to understand there is no other for you but the husband or wife you now have, I believe the marriage becomes *strong*. There will be less worrying about whether the marriage will last. Entertaining thoughts of being with someone else or separating from that companion does not even enter the mind. Do you get what I am saying? That *deep down feeling* and *knowing* that your spouse is the greatest partner for you and sensing the *rightness* of the relationship is "powerful." You grow and learn from each other.

Understanding, getting it, grasping the fact, embracing, and believing that your companion is "tops in your book" makes for a successful marriage. When you know you already have the best, you don't look for anything else.

Ralph, you are my "One and Only." I know there is no one else for me but you.

If we can get to the place where God is God ...Lord ...King ...Ruler ...the *only true God* for us, then we have a communion and relationship with Him that will not be broken. There is no other God! There are no multiple gods in this world; well, the world says there is, but the Word declares not so.

There is no God like my God. No one or nothing can do for me what He has done and continues to do for me everyday. He knows my needs and meets them. He understands me fully. He loves me in spite of my faults. He accepts me. He will never let go of my hand in this relationship because He wants to be with me *forever*!

I have known the Lord as my Savior since the age of six. If He didn't completely satisfy I would have gone looking for "something else" a long time ago. I have never thought about walking away from Him because there is no one else like Him. *He is God!* He honors me and loves me. He cherishes me and what we have will last.

> O Lord, there is none like thee, neither is there any God beside thee ...
>
> I Chronicles 17:20 (KJV)

> But the Lord is the true God, he is the living God, and an everlasting king ...
>
> Jeremiah 10:10 (KJV)

Dear children, keep away from anything that might take God's place in your hearts.

I John 5:21 (NLT)

And Jesus said unto them, I am the bread of life: he that cometh to me shall never hunger; and he that believeth on me shall never thirst.

John 6:35 (KJV)

Jealousy

We are all jealous to a certain degree. That may not be bad if it does not control or wreak havoc on our relationships. There is nothing wrong with having a "that's my man" or "that's my woman" mentality if it is wrapped up with respect and care. When jealousy gets out of hand, it is very dangerous and can destroy a relationship. That occurs when respect and trust is *not* part of a relationship.

Ralph is my man. He is not a flirt (except with me), and does not give me any reason to be jealous of him. I am not a flirt (except with him), and I do not give Ralph any reason to be jealous of me. That is so important, not giving our spouses reasons to be jealous.

People are not the only reasons for which we become jealous. It could simply come about because of what occupies your time. Excessive time on the job or with a hobby could make your spouse jealous.

I became jealous early in our marriage of Ralph's career. Working in retail meant spending a great deal of time around females. I remember walking in the store where Ralph was part of management, and there he sat with three or four female coworkers. I was so mad! He informed me before going to work that day that he would not be able to spare time to have lunch with me. I popped in unannounced, and there he sat. I was in shock! How long had this been going on? Jealousy breeds distrust, anguish and confusion over sometimes "nothing." Many times our perception of what we *see* is not what *is* (as was in this case).

I turned around and headed for the exit door. Ralph saw me and made a beeline for me. I was too hot to discuss or listen to what he had to say. After he got home from work, I had settled down enough to listen. Ralph had sat down to eat a sandwich for a few minutes and the female coworkers sat down at his table. He said, "What was I supposed to say … that they could not sit there … that my new bride wouldn't understand?" (And why could he not say that?) Anyway, it was a lesson I had to learn. Time has a way of helping us mature and trust one another in marriage.

I hear women speak of making their husbands jealous. When not getting enough attention from their spouse, perhaps this is the only thing they can come up with to remedy the situation. This will only make matters worse and could turn out differently than what was hoped. Determine to be a good wife, pay attention to your appearance, and take care of your man. Devotion pays off.

God is jealous over us with a "godly jealousy" the Bible says. This means He is hurt when anything or anyone takes His place in our lives. He has no problem with us giving time to our families, jobs, hobbies, etc. However, when we allow "things" and people to take all our time and He is left with very little of it, if any, it is hurtful.

His devotion to us is total, complete, pure, unselfish, and unlike anything we will ever experience with a human being. He wants us to be careful we do not place "everything else" before Him. Isn't that what we desire of our spouses ...just don't put everything or everyone before our marriage? That's what God is saying to us. Give me some time ...love Me ...commit to our relationship.

He gave His life for us. Surely we can spare some time for Him every single day. Don't get so busy with "life" that He is given the "leftovers" from the day. This is when you run the risk of letting "stuff" or "people" become your god. He deserves better. He is the only true God.

...for I the Lord thy God am a jealous God ...

Exodus 20:5 (KJV)

For thou shalt worship no other god: for the Lord, whose name is Jealous, is a jealous God.

Exodus 34:14 (KJV)

...I, the Lord your God, am a jealous God who will not tolerate your affection for any other gods ...

Deuteronomy 5:9 (NLT)

Yet I am the Lord thy God ...and thou shalt know no god but me: for there is no saviour beside me.

Hosea 13:4 (KJV)

The Day Is Not Lost

The sun was shining. One could not have asked for a more beautiful day for a picnic and hiking trip. I was ecstatic about the trip that Ralph, the boys, and I had planned for the day. However, before we even had the car packed for our outing, the clouds began to roll in and so did negative thoughts in my mind. With the appearance of those few clouds, my optimism also clouded rather quickly. But leave it to Ralph to save the day by saying, "Come on, let's go, it's just a few clouds. We've got the day ahead of us. Don't allow a few clouds to ruin our day." So I tried for the optimism again, loaded up the car and off we went.

Once we reached our destination, a light shower began to fall. There were no malls around or putt-putt, or any other "fun" things to do in sight. Ralph continued with the plans made, and did his best to assure me the day was not ruined. How often do we get to have a picnic in the back of a station wagon? We laid down the back seat of the car and all four of us crawled in as the hatchback door was lifted and we picnicked. What an experience! Just as we finished our lunch, the rain stopped. Can you believe it? Just in time for us to hike that mountain we had our eyes on. And we did. It was the most fun. I almost canceled our plans because of a few clouds that barged in on my otherwise cloudless sky. *Thanks, Ralph, for teaching me to make the most of every circumstance.*

How many times has our day just barely gotten started and the clouds rolled in? There may be problems on the job, kids get sick, or the dog gets loose again. And the first thought is, "If this is the way the rest of the day is going to be then I would just as soon go back to bed." God has taught me to settle down, stop what I'm doing, and take a "time-out" with Him.

Ask (if you haven't already) for Him to take charge, to order your day. He can get things rolling in the right direction again.

"Thank You, Lord, for helping me learn that valuable lesson …the day is not lost. You can salvage the morning or whatever is left of the day and make it good!"

Why am I discouraged? Why is my heart so sad? I will put my hope in God! I will praise him again—my Savior and my God!

Psalm 42:5 (NLT)

This is the day which the Lord hath made; we will rejoice and be glad in it.

Psalm 118:24 (KJV)

Teacher

One of the purposes for Ralph's life is that of a teacher. I believe he is a God-called teacher, meaning God has put a calling on his life to teach His Word. He started teaching Sunday school at a very young age and continues to do so.

With Ralph, teaching God's Word is a passion. Many teachers fill a position every Sunday because they enjoy it and the need for a teacher is there. Ralph has a need to teach, it is something he feels compelled by God to do.

I have witnessed hours upon hours that Ralph puts into studying a Sunday school lesson. He always has more material than he could possibly teach in the amount of time allotted to him *(Right, honey?)*. That is not necessarily a bad thing unless you go over your time limit, and this does happen with Ralph sometimes. He is just so into it ...

As one of his pupils in class, I sit under his teaching and can honestly say I learn something every time. I believe Ralph studies to teach himself and then imparts what he has found out to others. The Word will accomplish through the Spirit of God what it is supposed to as it finds the way to people's hearts and minds.

God's Word is life. Ralph makes the scriptures come alive through the Spirit of God working in him by studying and presenting the rich nuggets of truth. He teaches with enthusiasm and excitement that comes by the spirit of God living through him.

Ralph, let me be one that says I thoroughly enjoy your teaching the Word. Even if I am your wife, I can say you are truly my favorite teacher of the Word. The hours you pour over God's Word has paid off many times over because of the lives you touch. I hear it every Sunday, "Ralph did a good job teaching today, Ralph really brought home the lesson this Sunday to me in a real way, or Ralph was anointed by God in his teaching and I learned something that will help me." Keep up the good work, babe. The passion you have to "get into the Word" is not only enjoyed by those who hear, but you are also gaining great wisdom and knowledge from God.

This is definitely your purpose and calling. I am glad when we go to church every Sunday to hear God's Word.

God calls people to minister in different ways for Him. He may call you to minister the Word in message, sing songs for Him, work with children, visit the elderly in rest homes, work a puppet ministry, reach the youth and college age, teach in a marriage ministry, or serve in some other capacity within your church community.

We are to find joy in the Word because it is like finding great wealth—that's what the Bible tells us. The greatest Teacher of all is none other than the Holy Spirit of God. In fact, God sent His Spirit to come and teach us the Truth. Through God's Word, we come to know God and learn of Him and His ways. His Spirit brings the Word to memory after we have committed His Word to our heart by reading it or hearing it. Our faith is increased by hearing the Word. Great instructions are found there to help us live for God and lead others to Him.

Make time to get into God's Word by hearing a good Sunday school teacher, getting involved in a Bible study, or by listening to the sermons from a God-called minister. Your life and health (the whole man) will be blessed by this Truth taught to your soul.

I rejoice at thy word, as one that findeth great spoil.

Psalm 119:162 (KJV)

Give instruction to a wise man, and he will be yet wiser: teach a just man, and he will increase in learning.

Proverbs 9:9 (KJV)

Hear instruction, and be wise, and refuse it not.

Proverbs 8:33 (KJV)

But the Comforter, which is the Holy Ghost, whom the Father will send in my name, he shall teach you all things, and bring all things to your remembrance, whatsoever I have said unto you.

John 14:26 (KJV)

...thy word is truth.

John 17:17 (KJV)

...thou art a teacher come from God ...*(meaning Jesus)*

John 3:2 (KJV)

Keep My Commandments

Ralph thinks it is funny when he says, "If you love me, keep my commandments." I don't. Okay, we laugh about it, all because we know he is not serious. (*You are not serious, right?*)

I am so glad I did not marry someone who says, "Do as I say and not as I do." Ralph does not behave as a "lord" over me. He treats me the way he would like to be treated, for the most part.

Ralph makes suggestions and can be persuasive with those suggestions, but he is not a "ruler" over me. He is head of our family and that is quite different. I will go into that some other time. The term "lord" suggests having power and authority over others.

Women want to be treated with love, respect, and as

equals in intellect, capability, and competence. Oh, there are times when Ralph belittles me in some regard. Trust me; he is called "on the carpet." Let me just say I make him aware of how he is making me feel. My attitude is just as *rotten* as his in trying to make him aware he is not treating me as he should. We are both wrong when we allow ourselves to rise up against the other and try to force one another to feel less than we are. This happens in marriages, especially when we have expectations of our spouse that we do not apply to ourselves.

Ralph apologizes for belittling me (sometimes unaware of what he has done), and I apologize for being "mean-spirited" in trying to get my point across (no different than his belittling me). We get through it. We try to do better. Yeah, he walks off shaking his head and breathing something under his breath ... *What did you say, Ralph?* "Nothing, dear." *I believe I heard him say,* "Just keep my commandments ... that's all a man asks ... if you love me, just keep my commandments." *You are funny, Ralph ... in your own eyes!*

God *is* Lord. We must keep His commandments outlined in His Word. He *does* have power and authority over His children. That is not to be questioned, just understood. However, His lordship is unique in that He is loving, kind, respectful, mindful, caring, and trustworthy.

"Keep My commandments" is spoken throughout God's Word. We fare well or succeed when we put this into practice in our lives. We do not feel belittled, inferior or incompetent when following His rules. His Words and commands bring life and power to the soul and mind. His commandments do not make us angry when we hear them, as they totally enhance our relationship with Him and others.

A new commandment I give unto you, That ye love one another; as I have loved you, that ye also love one another.

John 13:34 (KJV)

For we will be counted as righteous when we obey all the commands the Lord our God has given us.

Deuteronomy 6:25 (NLT)

All he does is just and good, and all his commandments are trustworthy.

Psalm 111:7 (NLT)

He that hath my commandments, and keepeth them, he it is that loveth me: and he that loveth me shall be loved of my Father, and I will love him, and will manifest myself to him.

John 14:21 (KJV)

Those who obey God's commandments remain in fellowship with him, and he with them ...

I John 3:24 (NLT)

If ye love me, keep my commandments.

John 14:15 (KJV)

Living Your Faith

Recently, I have observed Ralph living his faith in a different way. He used to become disgruntled over a flat tire, forgetting something and having to go back to get it, or irritated at being held up in traffic. Now, Ralph takes those times to view God's hand in the matter. Perhaps, just perhaps, the time it takes to go back to the house to get the pager or cell phone prevents him from being in an accident. Who knows? He looks at these little delays as part of God's way of "keeping" Him.

If we say we trust God, then we should absolutely look at everything that happens to us as being part of His divine plan. Sometimes those "happenings" are frustrating and not pleasant, but in the overall picture it is His way of keeping His hand on our lives.

It is during these times we should try to relax and know

most likely it will not affect our day in the scope of things *that* much. *Ralph, it is nice to see you practice "taking it all in stride" compared to the way you used to react when having to backtrack or take a detour.*

Some delays put us in the path of people we would never come in contact with had things gone in a normal manner. It is soon evident we become the helping hand from God. Doesn't it make you feel good to help someone when they are in trouble? We have been in this situation many times, and "know" we were placed there.

I am trying to practice living my faith too. There are days Ralph and I do quite well at this. There are also those times we get frustrated and lose sight of our steps being ordered by God. However, it is the best way to live.

God knows what is best. We can absolutely sit back and thank God that some things just didn't work out the way we had planned! Have you ever passed an accident and knew you were within minutes of being in *that* accident had something not delayed you down the road? I have and I get goose bumps as I realize God is by my side.

God sees all. He is our protector. We pray for His hand of safety each day. Let's trust Him for this. Relax the next time something agitates you and keeps you from getting to your destination on time. Try seeing things differently—from His perspective. There is a reason for everything that happens. We may find out that reason, we may not.

If we are really going to trust God with our lives, we absolutely must relax and enjoy the ride He takes us on. Live your faith everyday. Pray this prayer:

...Thy will be done in earth, as it is in heaven.

Matthew 6:10 (KJV)

For in him we live, and move, and have our being ...

Acts 17:28 (KJV)

...It is no longer I who live, but Christ lives in me. So I live in this earthly body by trusting in the Son of God, who loved me and gave himself for me.

Galatians 2:20 (NLT)

...that thine hand might be with me, and that thou wouldest keep me from evil ...

I Chronicles 4:10 (KJV)

The Lord himself watches over you!

Psalm 121:5 (NLT)

Thoughtfulness

I met Ralph for lunch today. When he approached my car, I saw he had something in his hand. When he got inside he handed me a red "something." I unfolded the item and saw a Christmas stocking for our pet dog. I was thrilled to get this! I had wanted to get one during the Christmas season but did not want to pay the regular price. Today (January) Ralph saw one on clearance and bought it. Do you know what things like this do to women? It makes us giddy and glad and thankful for husbands that do *little* things. It was just the idea of Ralph taking the time to purchase a Christmas stocking for our dog that made me feel appreciated. He really could care less if the dog has a Christmas stocking or not (he does care for the dog), but because I wanted the stocking, he got one.

As far as getting gifts from Ralph, I don't like receiving flowers often. It is just the idea of paying money for something that will not last long. He has, however, bought me a couple of flower bouquets in the last six months "just because." I did like them! It was not my birthday or a special occasion. I had some friends ask me, "Why the flowers?" and I stated "Just because." Women like the "just because" stuff, guys. It's not even the gift, it is that we are being thought of.

I had a stomach virus for five days last week. I could not fix meals for my family and parents, which I try to do during the week. The first day of this illness, Ralph told me he would take care of supper for him and the guys. When he got home he stated he had taken a rotisserie turkey by my parents' home. That made me feel so good, just knowing he was thinking of me and how this would ease my mind about my parents being taken care of during mealtime.

Guys, you score way up there when thoughtful deeds are done "just because." Ladies, we should reciprocate in some way when things are done for us. Kindness begets kindness.

Ralph, your thoughtfulness is appreciated. I loved the doggy Christmas stocking!

Love is kind. God's love operating in our lives motivates us to want to do for others. God asks us to be mindful of others and we are to help out when we see a need. Doing for others is doing unto God. We are rewarded when we reach out and serve other people. I do believe it comes back to us in some way.

As God's children, the Word tells us we will "bear fruit" and there will be evidence of certain characteristics in our lives that we are His. This just lets people know that God is in us, and this is what causes us to be kind, good, loving, gentle, caring, and helpful people. Surprise someone today and do something for them "just because." It is a good feeling for you and the one you help.

> If someone has enough money to live well and sees a brother or sister in need but shows no compassion—how can God's love be in that person?

I John 3:17 (NLT)

> Since God chose you to be the holy people he loves, you must clothe yourselves with tenderhearted mercy, kindness, humility, gentleness, and patience.

Colossians 3:12 (NLT)

Let your light so shine before men, that they may see your good works, and glorify your Father, which is in heaven.

Matthews 5:16 (KJV)

For I was hungry, and you fed me. I was thirsty, and you gave me drink. I was a stranger, and you invited me into your home. I was naked, and you gave me clothing. I was sick, and you cared for me. I was in prison, and you visited me. Then these righteous ones will reply, "Lord, when did we ever see you hungry and feed you? Or thirsty and give you something to drink? Or a stranger and show you hospitality? Or naked and gave you clothing? When did we ever see you sick or in prison and visit you?" And the King will say, "I tell you the truth, when you did it to one of the least of these my brothers and sisters, you were doing it to me!"

Matthew 25:35–40 (NLT)

Forgiveness

Forgiveness is a must in a marriage. Sometimes it is easy to do and other times it's downright hard. Ralph and I have wrestled with this at different times in our marriage. There have been times we wondered if we could forgive the offence by the other. As far as I know, we always have forgiven the other. If there is something not forgiven, it will eventually find its way out. *Watch out, Ralph, I feel a historical moment coming on (just joking ... at least for now).*

We get our feelings hurt. Sometimes we are just too sensitive. I am more sensitive than Ralph. Yet, there are those occasions when I know I hurt him deeply. The boys have offended their father and me. We have caused emotional pain to our boys. It is unavoidable in a household, but we must know how to deal with it.

We know when we have offended our spouses. It does not feel good to know you have caused emotional pain, especially to those you love. There are times we are unaware we have offended, but I believe that is not often.

Ralph is fairly quick to say he is sorry when he offends me. I am a little less quick to say I am sorry. Is that because I have far fewer reasons to be sorry? That I am right more often? I wish!

Forgiveness. It is going to be needed sooner than you think. Be prepared by being quick to apologize if necessary when the other person feels offended. Many times space or time can help alleviate the hurtful situation, and the apology and forgiveness comes shortly thereafter.

Much of getting offended and being hurtful will lessen as we grow older and mature. I have arrived! Well, not really ...

God's Word has much to say about forgiveness. God forgives us of our sins. He expects forgiveness from us in our relationships with others. We must keep in mind His forgiveness every time we are offended. If we do this, it is much easier to forgive.

Holding grudges is damaging to our relationship with God and others. As stated above, sometimes forgiving is easy, and other times it proves to be so difficult that we wonder if we can. We can! God forgave! We can forgive as He does. He will enable us to do this. We will become stronger in our relationship with Him and the one we offend or are offended by. There will be times when we ask someone to forgive us and they refuse our apology. Our apology sets us free in our own spirit before God. The other party will have to answer God if they choose not to forgive. Forgiving is freeing. It is a command from God. It is the right thing to do.

...forgive, and ye shall be forgiven.

Luke 6:37 (KJV)

For thou, Lord, art good, and ready to forgive ...

Psalm 86:5 (KJV)

But if you refuse to forgive others, your Father will not forgive your sins.

Matthew 6:15 (NLT)

Then Peter came to him and asked, "Lord, how often should I forgive someone who sins against me? Seven times?" "No, not seven times," Jesus replied, "but seventy times seven!" (This simply means forgive as many times as necessary ... not just 490 times.)

Matthew 18:21, 22 (NLT)

And be ye kind one to another, tenderhearted, forgiving one another, even as God for Christ's sake hath forgiven you.

Ephesians 4:32 (KJV)

Make allowance for each other's faults, and forgive anyone who offends you. Remember, the Lord forgave you, so you must forgive others.

Colossians 3:13 (NLT)

This is a very serious matter of which I am about to write. The following is the biblical method to handle forgiveness and feeling wronged by a fellow believer.

If another believer sins against you, go privately and point out the offense. If the other person listens and confesses it, you have won that person back. But if you are unsuccessful, take one or two others with you and go back again, so that everything you say may be confirmed by two or three witnesses. If the person still refuses to listen, take your case to the church. Then if he or she won't accept the church's decision, treat that person as a pagan or a corrupt tax collector.

Matthew 18:15–17 (NLT)

This is biblical. If we do things in this fashion, the majority of the time it will never have to reach the church. Christians should be able to forgive and work through their differences. In rare cases we see the situation brought before the church and settled in this manner. Isn't God amazing in how He can bring about forgiveness in our hearts!

Are You On My Side?

I have gone a few rounds with Ralph in our married life asking this question, "Are you on my side or not?" For some reason, I felt it was carved in stone that you had to back up your companion 100% on *everything* in *every* situation! However, Ralph does not see it *my* way.

Ralph simply believes if he sees things the way I do, then yeah, he is on my side. If he does not see things the way I do he is still on my side but makes clear, "I just do not agree, *dear.*"

How dare he not back me up on a matter? Why don't you go "to bat" for me? It is funny after being married these twenty-five years that I have finally gotten this. I used to think he was *rejecting* me when he did not receive my opinion as his own. Was I arrogant or what, thinking I had the right perspective every single time something came up in our household? That is hard to admit (whew, got that over).

I do not take Ralph disagreeing with me personally any more. I have learned he has view points I must consider, and cannot feel attacked when they are unlike my own.

Thanks, Ralph, for loving me no matter what. When you do not take my side on a subject this in no way means you love me any less. You are simply stating how you feel and it is okay for me to feel another way. (Of course, if I feel real strongly, I may keep working on you to see it my way). Okay ... I know when to drop it ...

In the spiritual world, we must take a stand of whose side we are on. Either we accept God or we reject Him. There is no middle ground. By not choosing, we make a choice to reject God.

Life is good with God on our side. We still have pain, sorrow and troubles to face, but it sure is easier to go through these things knowing we have Him to help us.

...Who is on the Lord's side? ...

Exodus 32:26 (KJV)

...then choose today whom you will serve ...But as for me and my family, we will serve the Lord.

Joshua 24:15 (NLT)

Today, I have given you the choice between life and death, between blessings and curses. Now I call on heaven and earth to witness the choice you make. Oh, that you would choose life, so that you and your descendants might live! You can make this choice by loving the Lord your God, obeying him, and committing yourself firmly to him. This is the key to your life. And if you love and obey the Lord, you will live long ...

Deuteronomy 30:19, 20 (NLT)

The Lord is on my side; I will not fear: what can man do unto me?

Psalm 118:6 (KJV)

...this I know; for God is for me.

Psalm 56:9 (KJV)

Healing Balm

Love letters …ladies, we enjoy getting them. Ralph is a great writer when he gets inspired. We wrote many letters to each other while dating and I have kept them all. Ralph continues to write letters, or mainly in cards now, but they serve as a great help in our marriage. I write back, of course.

Reading love letters are a great "pick me up" when you feel down. I get my stack out from time to time and just begin to read. Pretty soon, my feelings of "being down" are gone just because I am reading words that Ralph has written for me. These words encourage. They make me feel wonderful about myself. You can't stay down when you read words that tell you how beautiful you are and loving and funny and great. I could just go on and on. (I must stop …I am embarrassing myself!)

Being reminded of good stuff about yourself and your relationship is what rereading the love letters are about. It is a good place to start if you realize your relationship with your spouse is not where it should be. The letters frame in your mind pictures of great memories and how it can be again.

Maybe you have not received or written love letters. Now is a good time to start. Words are powerful and can be called on time and again to evoke feelings that may be dying out. Words written to our spouses stir up *what is already there* and starts the relationship back on the road to healing.

Ralph, are you feeling inspired? It is about time for another love letter or card, don't you think? Or are you waiting on me? That can be remedied ... I feel inspiration coming on. Thanks, Ralph, for all the words of encouragement and love written to me that serve a great purpose in my life today.

We will experience down times in our lives. Sometimes we can pinpoint why and other times we just don't know why we feel lousy. You can do something about this: Get God's Word and begin to read of His love for you and how He thinks on you. It will not be long before those words that hold *life* and *power* will smooth over your soul, heart, and mind like a healing balm. God's Word is *power* to His children. Read them often. Need a "pick me up" today? Get to reading!

Your promise revives me; it comforts me in all my troubles.

Psalm 119:50 (NLT)

Heaviness in the heart of man maketh it stoop: but a good word maketh it glad.

Proverbs 12:25 (KJV)

Let the word of Christ dwell in you richly in all wisdom; teaching and admonishing one another in psalms and hymns and spiritual songs, singing with grace in your hearts to the Lord.

Colossians 3:16 (KJV)

...Let thine heart retain my words: keep my commandments, and live.

Proverbs 4:4 (KJV)

How sweet your words taste to me; they are sweeter than honey.

Psalm 119:103 (NLT)

...the words that I speak unto you, they are spirit, and they are life. (words spoken by Jesus)

John 6:63 (KJV)

Borrow No Trouble

Ralph will not and does not speculate about anything. He does not spend energy and time on "guessing" outcomes or future developments that he possibly cannot know. I, on the other hand, speculate more than I should. I spend way too much time trying to figure out the end result, the possibility, the what ifs, and whatevers.

Setting goals and planning is definitely part of Ralph's makeup, but he will just not take on "stuff" that is not meant to be taken on at the present. He does not tell me in so many words to "get a life," but gently suggests putting all the guesswork aside. (Whatever!)

Ralph has talked about a couple of matters with me concerning "the unknown." He has made me aware of the location of important papers should something ever happen to him. He also has talked with me about protecting myself *should* someone break into our home since I am there most hours of the day. A man came to the door of our house recently and just looked suspicious to me (that doesn't take much effort on my part). Our dog, Winston, ferocious as he sounds, is quite timid and shy. You never know, he could do a good job at protecting me if necessary (hope I never find out). I told Ralph if someone broke in, I would probably forget anything he has suggested to me.

Otherwise, Ralph takes on the day. He does not examine everything to death. I try to force his hand many times to *just tell me* what he thinks *might* happen down the road about certain situations. He tells me, "I just don't know."

I am learning to take life one day at a time. It sure is much easier than worrying about things we have no control over and may never confront anyway.

Ralph, your example of "not wondering" about tomorrow and its cares is saving some years off my life!

God is in control. How many times have we heard that? Do you believe it? Do you live it? We all have some trouble with "guesswork" and day-to-day living. It can be difficult not to bring "tomorrow's problems" into today's agenda. The Bible says we are not to worry about tomorrow's troubles; we have enough of that to think on for today.

Many of the unknowns will never materialize for us to have to deal with, so we do waste precious time by this unprofitable thinking. Ask God to help you abandon all the speculating to Him, and deal with what lies clearly at hand.

So don't worry about tomorrow, for tomorrow will bring its own worries. Today's trouble is enough for today!

Matthew 6:34 (NLT)

Give all your worries and care to God, for he cares about you.

I Peter 5:7 (NLT)

Fighting Our Battles

Ralph enjoys "rough-housing" with the boys. They have engaged in this since the boys were small. Now, it has turned into quite a competition since our guys are seventeen and twenty years old.

It used to be when the boys were younger and they picked a little fight with their dad that they would find me and hide behind me. I was to *protect* them from this "big man."

Now, the fights are not so little and have taken on new meaning—every man for himself!

Recently, I heard Ralph and our youngest son, Zach (now seventeen) battling in the other room. I heard the loud noises that go along with their fighting for about five minutes until it was really getting on my last, good nerve. I raised my voice and simply said, "Enough!"

I was surprised how quickly the noise stopped, and I assumed the rough-housing as well. Good. They listened. I wish I could say that was the end of it. However, I heard a small groan and could tell it was coming from Zach. I dismissed it. I put out of mind another groan until Zach's noises tipped me off that the fighting had not stopped as I had demanded. I got up from working in my office. Ralph had Zach in a "head lock" and they were going at it as quietly as possible. It was a sight to behold! You know the first person I came down on? Brandon, our twenty-year-old son. I came down on him because he was simply watching the show with this huge grin on his face. He was just as guilty for being in the room and clearly being amused by what was going on. Let's just say I put a stop to it all. After all, Ralph could get hurt (*Sorry, Ralph. I have to call it like I see it!*). I also worried about Zach being *crushed* by "the big man" in some way too!

They enjoy these father-son fights. I think they are stupid. They will continue them for years to come I suspect.

Battles are fought every day in our minds. Some of the

battles can be fought fairly easily, and others require help from God. Mind battles, you know, the "trouble" that digs and picks and causes despair to grip us. You may feel hope is gone and there is no way out of "this one."

God will fight your battles right along with you. He never leaves us unprotected or by ourselves. We must guard our minds by having the "mind of Christ," which simply means we are to become like him in our nature and act as He would. Renew your mind; give it a break from all the disturbing thoughts trying to invade it by "getting into the Word." It works!

...But we have the mind of Christ.

I Corinthians 2:16 (KJV)

Let this mind be in you, which was also in Christ Jesus:

Philippians 2:5 (KJV)

Therefore, put on every piece of God's armor so you will be able to resist the enemy in the time of evil. Then after the battle you will still be standing firm. Stand your ground, putting on the belt of truth and the body armor of God's righteousness. For shoes, put on the peace that comes from the Good News so that you will be fully pre-pared. In addition to all of these, hold up the shield of faith to stop the fiery arrows of the devil. Put on salvation as your helmet, and take the sword of the Spirit, which is the word of God.

Ephesians 6:13–17 (NLT)

Put on your new nature, and be renewed as you learn to know your Creator and become like him.

Colossians 3:10 (NLT)

So letting your sinful nature control your mind leads to death. But letting the Spirit control your mind leads to life and peace.

Romans 8:6 (NLT)

And be renewed in the spirit of your mind;

Romans 4:23 (KJV)

Divided Houses Fall

I have observed families living chaotic lives. It seems they thrive in being disorganized and confused. They do not know how to get along and unite as a family. Strife and arguing and yelling and tension are normal for these families.

We are aware of times of being harsh and argumentative with one another in our family life. We discuss it and change it. If this is allowed to continue the "family" is weakened by disorder and it will not be long before respect, organization, and caring one for the other "leaves the house."

Ralph and I know if we do not get along with one another then shortly the boys will pick up on our "tension" and react the same way. Chaos breeds more of the same. I am so thankful we understand the importance of "nipping this in the bud," as a well-known TV deputy sheriff stated. It just cannot be allowed to continue or the household will suffer greatly.

This unity starts with the husband and wife. We must seek to come to agreement when we differ on matters in the household or with our children. We set the example before our kids in this. They will learn quickly how to work out their differences when they see it modeled by their parents.

Sarcasm, in my opinion, when allowed without boundaries, is deadly in a marriage. Ralph and I observed a young married couple several years back. The husband was very sarcastic towards his wife …all the time. He may have meant it to be funny, but there comes a time when sarcasm has to go. Ralph and I got into that "sarcasm thing" early on in our marriage, and it did not take long before we realized we had to stop. We did the sarcastic talk "in fun," but gained understanding very shortly that it was tearing at our respect for one another. I feel strongly about this subject. If this is part of your relationship, you might want to think again and eradicate it from your speech. Build up one another!

Unity is something we should pray and strive for in our families and communities and church life. Getting along with others should be important to us. This is important to God, as He talks of this subject in His word. We can accomplish many things in our lives if we unite together instead of pulling against one another. Family, community, and church will be strong if we practice unity. Being in harmony with one another is not always easy. Anytime you have people gathered together, there are diversities of thoughts, ways of doing things and very different backgrounds present. We need God to help unite us and know how to *agree to disagree* if necessary.

...Every kingdom divided against itself is brought to desolation; and every city or house divided against itself shall not stand:

Matthew 12:25 (KJV)

How wonderful and pleasant it is when brothers live together in harmony!

Psalm 133:1 (NLT)

Make every effort to keep yourselves united in the Spirit, binding yourselves together with peace.

Ephesians 4:3 (NLT)

Do all that you can to live in peace with everyone.

Romans 12:18 (NLT)

In the The Day of Trouble

About 6:30 a.m., I go to plug up a little heater in an outlet behind our couch. I turned up the thermostat on the heat in our home, but I love to get by my little heater in the wintertime. So, I plug the heater into the outlet and my weight pushed against the couch and caught my arm ... tight! I tried *everything* to get my arm loose from between the couch and the wall. Nothing was working. Ralph and the boys were sleeping in that morning.

I don't recall the amount of time I spent trying to get my arm out from behind the couch, but I do recall I was beginning to experience pain. Our bedroom is quite a ways from where I was being held captive. However, I thought if I could just get Ralph's attention, he could move out the couch and free my arm and I would be okay.

I decided on a loud whisper to get Ralph's attention so I would not wake the boys. I mean, after all, I am *super embarrassed* that I have my arm wedged between the couch and the wall to begin with! I loudly whispered, "Ralph, Ralph, do you hear me? Ralph, I have my arm caught behind the couch." I hear nothing.

My whispers became a little louder. I used my regular tone of voice this time, saying, "Ralph, Ralph, I need your help" …still, nothing from my "knight." Now, I'm going to tell it like it is: I started to hurt …bad!

Forget the whispers, forget the regular tone of voice, I now shouted, "Somebody help me!" That got everybody's attention (probably the neighbors as well). Here comes Ralph and the boys running to my aid. Ralph approaches with his face all scrunched up from being sound asleep and asks, "What's wrong?" I told him I had my arm wedged behind the couch and could not get out. Did I miss something here? He and the boys started laughing hysterically! Again, did I miss something that was supposed to be funny?

Well, my hero got me out! We still talk of this today. The boys and Ralph will never understand the pressure on my arm that day (don't even start the violin music here), but that's okay. I know of the pain. I am glad they finally came to my rescue, but next time *hurry up!*

Jesus invites us to call on Him in the day of trouble. He hears the *first* time we ask. He comes to our rescue time and again.

Are we guilty of calling on everybody else before we remember to call on His Name? He is never too busy and is absolutely available *every time* you call out to Him.

Whatever kind of help we need, He offers and provides. Don't be afraid to ask for His help—small or large. He will not laugh at you, even though others may think your request or situation is ridiculous. Everything that matters to you matters to God.

Are you in trouble? Do you need help at this moment? You don't even have to holler to be heard. Just a simple "Help me, Lord" will do. Now, that's what I call coming to our rescue!

> Hide not thy face from me in the day when I am in trouble; incline thine ear unto me: in the day when I call answer me speedily.

> Psalm 102:2 (KJV)

The Lord is good, a strong refuge when trouble comes. He is close to those who trust in him.

Nahum 1:7 (NLT)

The Lord hears his people when they call to him for help. He rescues them from all their troubles.

Psalm 34:17 (NLT)

When they call on me, I will answer; I will be with them in trouble. I will rescue and honor them.

Psalm 91:15 (NLT)

For I the Lord thy God will hold thy right hand, saying unto thee, Fear not; I will help thee.

Isaiah 41:13 (KJV)

Do Not Be Ashamed

We all know people who are supposed to be our friends. There are those times when in a crowd those same people completely ignore you or act as though you are not even an acquaintance of theirs, let alone a friend. Is that aggravating or what?

Ralph and the boys think it is hilarious at a restaurant when we get up to leave and they act as if they do not know me. They linger behind while I get up from my seat and start walking out. When I look back to find out what is taking them so long, they are deliberately keeping their distance and snickering. I know what is coming, so I don't *even* play along with their silly game. I just continue to walk out with my head held high and completely ignore their remarks of "not knowing this lady!" I must say it is funny … sometimes.

Ralph, I am not sure if you are the instigator of this or not, but you are guilty by going along with it. Well, sticks and stones may break my bones, but your actions and foolishness will not hurt me!

I told you Ralph had a dry sense of humor; this is just an example of such.

For those who know God, *know* Him at all times, with all people, wherever you are. This is important. God takes very seriously being *our* God. He is hurt when we act as though we do not know Him at certain times. If you are constantly doing this around certain people, then you may need to change who you call your friends. It should never be in question in our friends' minds if we are children of God or not.

God loves you. Love Him. Don't be embarrassed of this relationship you have in Him.

Show it, talk it, live it 24/7. I must include what God's Word tells us about what will happen when we deny God before others. Read on to find out His response.

> For I am not ashamed of the gospel of Christ: for it is the power of God unto salvation to every one that believeth …

Romans 1:16 (KJV)

For I fully expect and hope that I will never be ashamed, but that I will continue to be bold for Christ ...

Philippians 1:20 (NLT)

So never be ashamed to tell others about our Lord ...

2 Timothy 1:8 (NLT)

If anyone is ashamed of me and my message in these adulterous and sinful days, the Son of Man will be ashamed of that person when he returns in the glory of his Father with the holy angels.

Mark 8:38 (NLT)

I tell you the truth, everyone who acknowledges me publicly here on earth, the Son of Man will also acknowledge in the presence of God's angels. But anyone who denies me here on earth will be denied before God's angels.

Luke 12:8, 9 (NLT)

Focus On Me

Ralph called and told me he had just gone over an embankment in the car but was okay. I felt sick to my stomach. My youngest son and I went to him. When we arrived at the accident scene, I saw where he had landed. I started trembling. It was by God's grace he was walking around outside of the car. His car landed at a railroad track. We were at the accident scene for approximately two hours. He was able to get the car out with the aid of our son and a couple of guys, driving it down alongside the railroad track to get up to the highway.

The car in front of Ralph had made an abrupt stop, as the car in front of that person had done the same thing. Ralph veered off the side of the road to keep from hitting the vehicle in front of him. He caught the side of a telephone pole as he went down the embankment.

We went back to the scene the next day. Then he saw it—a teddy bear dressed in a clown costume up in a tree. He remembered then that the clown had gotten his attention the day before and he had glanced over to see what it was. That tiny glance of taking his eyes off of what was important (the road and vehicles ahead) caused him to wreck. He never mentioned the clown until the day we revisited that area. I had not seen the clown the two hours I had been all around that place the day before. Was it there or was it not there the day he wrecked? Since then, I have teased him mercilessly about this. I am sure it was there and had caught his attention when he veered off the side of the road. It is odd we both did not remember seeing the clown the time we spent getting his car out of the embankment. I guess we had other things on our minds. However, there it was the next day for all to see. Oh well ...

Focus is important in all we do, especially in our Christian walk. It is so easy to get our eyes off Jesus and on circumstances surrounding us. When we allow "things" to grasp our attention from God, we grow panicky, get into trouble, and soon lose sight of our direction. It is then we must put forth effort to turn our eyes *back* on Jesus. We do this by calling out to Him, reading His word and thinking "right thoughts" during times of difficulty. It is not long before our focus becomes clear again and we feel safe in proceeding in whatever we are doing.

Just a glance, just merely taking our eyes off the One who directs our path can be devastating. When this happens, we must center our attention back on Who is in control, and not what is going on around us. Read the example of Peter in the Bible and how he took his eyes off the Savior. He allowed "the winds and waves" to consume his thoughts and change the course God had started. However, he did cry out for help:

> Then Peter called to him, "Lord, if it's really you, tell me to come to you, walking on the water." "Yes, come," said Jesus. So Peter went over the side of the boat and walked on the water toward Jesus. But when he saw the strong wind and the waves, he was terrified and began to sink. "Save me, Lord!" he shouted. Jesus immediately reached out and grabbed him ...

> Matthew 14:28 (NLT)

Help was there. Peter was saved when he turned his eyes back on Jesus and he took the hand offered. Accept your help today! God has His hand stretched out to you to get you back on course again, just take it.

When Disappointment Comes

We are not strangers to disappointments. They are inevitable, so I am trying to learn how to respond to them.

Ralph and I faced a very disappointing time in our lives several years ago. I will not go into the details of the matter but we felt *crushed*, and I almost allowed it to get the best of me.

I was so sure of a matter, just *knew* we were in God's perfect will. I was completely confident that this situation was working out for our best. I told *everybody*! I knew the outcome was going to be what we anticipated. I could not have been more *wrong* when the end result was realized.

I was so hurt. I told the Lord that "He looked bad." I had told everyone of how He was working in our behalf and now He looked bad. I know that was awful for me to say. However, I felt defeated, betrayed, abandoned—you name it, I felt it. Ralph did too. Only he could look at things more objectively (thank God) than I. It is a great help when your spouse can be confident and positive when you are down. He shared with me that what happened, happened. God allowed it to work out that way. He told me I had a choice: to accept the outcome and move on or admit defeat and allow my relationship with God to suffer. More importantly, if I continued on in such bitterness, I could permit my relationship with God to be severed because He chose a different answer than I had desired. I chose to accept God's working in the matter and moved on. I now see why. God was working and just a few months later a "better thing" for us occurred. Sometimes He holds out giving us something that we perceive as *good* because He has something *better* in mind.

Now, Ralph is facing disappointment in his life. He has expected and waited for an answer to a request for almost a year, and nothing has materialized. He was so close in seeing this happen on two occasions. But nothing. It is hard for him and now it is my turn to encourage and help him through this disappointing time.

Thanks, Ralph, for being strong when I am weak. I hope

I am there for you in the same way you are for me. We will have more disappointments to face. Let's continue to be there for the other with the right words, prayer, and commitment to see each other through.

It is downright hard to expect and hope for a certain outcome in an area of our lives and then nothing further from that expectation is seen. The sting from that blow is sometimes piercing to the point you cannot seem to get beyond the "I can't believe this is the way it turned out!"

Sometimes we see why and know that it is better for things to turn out the way they do. Other times, it will be the hardest thing to abandon our expectation and turn in another direction. It may seem like our heart breaks in a million pieces and it is just not possible to pull through *this one.* I encourage you to stand still and know He is God. Simply stop ... do not push the matter any further. Run to God instead of away from Him. Fall into His embrace and He will comfort and strengthen you as only He can. He knows what is best! We only think we do. Let go, permit, allow and give clearance to the Lord to do what is *right* in your life. The sooner you can do this, the faster you will heal and the quicker you will experience "the better" He has planned for you.

Be still, and know that I *am* God ...

Psalm 46:10 (KJV)

Being confident of this very thing, that he which hath begun a good work in you will perform *it* until the day of Jesus Christ.

Philippians 1:6 (KJV)

They do not fear bad news; they confidently trust the Lord to care for them.

Psalm 112:7 (NLT)

When the storms of life come, the wicked are whirled away, but the godly have a lasting foundation.

Proverbs 10:25 (NLT)

Trust in the Lord with all thine heart; and lean not unto thine own understanding.

Proverbs 3:5 (KJV)

And we know that God causes everything to work together for the good of those who love God and are called according to his purpose for them.

Romans 8:28 (NLT)

Come To Me

There are days when I need to bear my soul and Ralph allows me to do so. He knows when I just need to talk things out. He sits there and listens, nods, makes the appropriate expressions, and responses to let me know he is following me. *(You are following me, right?)*

Talk about good therapy! Ralph knows when to put in an "uh-huh, yeah, I know" so that I am aware he is paying attention. *(You are paying attention, right?)* He has learned when he does this, I won't have to play twenty questions …you know, when we try to get our partners to repeat what we've said. In response, our poor husbands stutter nervously because they don't have a clue! *(That's not you, right?)*

Part of meeting my needs (as a woman) is allowing me to sit down once in a while (okay, quite often) and spill my entire gamut of thoughts and feelings to my spouse. It helps. I'm not asking him to fix it …just listen.

Thanks, Ralph, for listening. (You are listening, right?) It's good to have a partner with whom I can share everything. Thanks for not watching the clock or signaling that you are in a hurry or bored with what I am saying. (You're not bored, right?)

No one can give 100%, complete, total attention like Jesus. We humans are guilty of listening with one ear and trying to figure out what we are going to say next. Perhaps we become bored with the conversation or we feel totally helpless as our partners and friends share their concerns. We squirm and jiggle the change in our pockets and inadvertently send the message that we do not care, nor have the time.

Jesus extends an invitation to come and lay our burdens on Him—where we can find rest. It is great to talk to Jesus without interruptions or being made to feel pressed for time.

When troubled or aggravated, just taking a few moments to talk it over with God makes everything clearer. He *can* fix it and soothe our troubled souls.

Then Jesus said, Come to me, all of you who are weary and carry heavy burdens, and I will give you rest.

Matthew 11:28 (NLT)

The Lord hears his people when they call to him for help. He rescues them from all their troubles.

Psalm 34:17 (NLT)

But God did listen! He paid attention to my prayer.

Psalm 66:19 (NLT)

Consistency

There are people whose very moods change as frequently and easily as a chameleon changes color with its surroundings. We've all come in contact with such people and are not sure if we should speak or remain silent for fear they may be in the middle of one of their "mood swings."

It is very refreshing to have a companion who is consistent in mood and temperament. I am sure he feels fear, dread, worry, and other emotions like I do when changes suddenly occur. Ralph deals with the changes and seldom allows the upsets to give him the freedom to react harshly. I know this has to come from God. Ralph's constant respect and love is still intact even when his surroundings are in a tailspin.

Ralph, I am so glad I don't have to worry if I should speak or be quiet until I decipher your mood. What a relief to know you are the same loving man every single day and are approachable from one day to the next.

I'm striving to improve in this area. Sometimes I may give a chameleon a "run for his money" when my emotions take a roller coaster ride. (I won't *even* blame such emotional upheaval on being a woman either!)

We need an anchor that will keep us from drifting aimlessly in this fast-changing world. While we face constant change, sometimes it can catch us off guard. We can become exasperated, frustrated, hopeless, overwhelmed, and burnt out.

Jesus is our anchor in this world. We never have to worry if He is approachable. He is steadfast, sure, solid—a firm foundation that does not give when everything around us begins to shift. He is the balance in our lives. No matter how hard life's boat may rock from the crashing waves, Jesus is on board and He does not change! Take comfort in having this kind of stability.

Jesus Christ the same yesterday, and to day, and for ever.

Hebrews 13:8 (KJV)

For I am the Lord, I change not ...

Malachi 3:6 (KJV)

My God is my rock, in whom I find protection. He is my shield, the power that saves me, and my place of safety. He is my refuge, my savior, the one who saves me from violence.

2 Samuel 22:3 (NLT)

No Secrets

Kids have been known to think parents have eyes in the back of their heads. You don't get by much with Ralph. Ralph is very observant and picks up on any changes made (be it in myself, the house, or the kids; he even knows when the dog gets a new toy).

I share everything and am not one to keep a secret from Ralph. Even when the boys get into trouble, I inform him and we work things out together. Whatever happens in my life, Ralph knows it *all*. There may be some things he would prefer not to know but he does.

It's great when your companion knows all, then you don't have to worry about being "found out" when you spend more than you should, put the dent in the car, or accept an invitation to the last place your husband would want to go (even though he is informed at the last possible moment ... sorry).

Ralph's mindfulness of what goes on in our household shows he is in tune with us. I don't see it as being "nosey" or "controlling." Anyway, he knows pretty much all that's going on, except for ... (*Just teasing, Ralph!*)

We cannot keep a secret from God, as He knows everything, sees everything, is everywhere, and it will always be this way.

God keeps track of you every moment of every day. Don't think you are ever left alone for one second. His Word is a great reminder of how much He is in tune with everything we do. That is how excellent His care is.

We can feel good about "discussing anything" in prayer with God. He already knows, but wants us to come to Him. Take all your burdens, prayer requests and praises to Him. I find it reassuring that He is "watching over me."

> For the eyes of the Lord run to and fro throughout the whole earth, to shew himself strong in the behalf of them whose heart is perfect toward him ...

2 Chronicles 16:9 (KJV)

O Lord, you have examined my heart and know everything about me. You know when I sit down or stand up. You know my thoughts even when I'm far away. You see me when I travel and when I rest at home. You know everything I do. You know what I am going to say even before I say it, Lord. You go before me and follow me. You place your hand of blessing on my head. Such knowledge is too wonderful for me, too great for me to understand. (You must read this entire chapter to get full understanding of His care for you.)

Psalm 139:1–6 (NLT)

...for he hath said, I will never leave thee, nor forsake thee.

Hebrews 13:5 (KJV)

Sticks Closer Than a Brother

Ralph once sat by my side while I worked on a Board Certification project for a prestigious psychologist. My job was to transcribe the doctor's notes and the end result would be a written presentation for the Board to review. This was done on a word processor (not the great computers we have available to us now).

I had worked for two solid weeks on this Board Certification. The timing for this was not one I would have chosen ...the Christmas season. The final revisions were marked on the already typed pages I had turned in previously to the doctor. When I got the final revisions in my hands, I absolutely felt I could not go through the eighty-plus pages one more time. I had already put in so many hours (I still had other doctors' work to transcribe each day). I felt overwhelmed!

Ralph was getting ready to leave on a business trip out of town and here I was, totally out of it. He pulled up a chair beside my office desk and calmly stated, "Okay, babe, let's take one page at a time and we'll get through this." He was my constant companion for the next six to seven hours. I have told him how much I appreciated his help, but I am not sure he fully understands what he did for me.

By the time he had to leave on his business trip, I had completed a little over half of the work. When he got to the hotel, he called to see how things were shaping up. Just to hear his voice made me feel tons better. When I had him beside me those several hours and knowing I was still in his thoughts at 1:30 a.m. (when I finally completed the manuscript) meant more to me than he will ever know.

Ralph couldn't do the work for me, but he was there literally for a lot of it and supported me with comforting words when he couldn't be there in person.

When we are involved in difficult tasks we can know that Jesus is our constant companion, and that makes tackling the job a lot easier. What a mistake it is not to invite His presence in *all* we do. He, joyfully, will be right there, seeing us through and offering His strength in small (and big) ways that cannot be overlooked.

I give many thanks to You, Lord, for being by my side. It's certainly wonderful to know You are with me today, and equally so to know You are there for me all my days.

People may not always be there for us physically, but Jesus *can* and *will* be there! I can count on Him. He is not bound by time, jobs, business trips, or other things that prevent you and me from being there for each other.

…and there is a friend that sticketh closer than a brother.

Proverbs 18:24 (KJV)

…for he hath said, I will never leave thee, nor forsake thee.

Hebrews 13:5 (KJV)

God is our refuge and strength, a very present help in trouble.

Psalm 46:1 (KJV)

On Nurturing Relationships

Early on in our marriage, Ralph told me that he would never be satisfied with our relationship. How would you feel if you were told such a thing? I received this bit of news in a letter he wrote. When I came to that part of the letter, I stopped and reflected on what he had said. I did not get upset, throw the letter away, or discontinue reading (the thought crossed my mind). However, I knew Ralph well enough that he had a good reason for making such a statement.

He went on to explain that he would never be satisfied with our marriage, as he feels we could always do something more, something different to improve upon what is already good. I agree.

There are times in our marriage that we allow our relationship to become dull and unexciting, perhaps routine.

It is not too long before I reflect back on that letter and realize that *I*, as well as *he*, should do something to make our relationship better. A marriage and love gone sour is the result of a relationship left unattended.

Thank you, Ralph. That letter continues to stick with me. I know that you did not mean that you are unhappy with what we have, but you feel that when one stops trying to improve their relationship then it suffers.

Jesus truly does His part in the relationship with His children. His forgiveness, faithfulness, mercy, and love are consistent and working components in our daily lives.

Our relationship with Jesus can go awry and lose its satisfaction and fulfillment. This happens when we slack off in our communication with Him (prayer), when we fail to listen to Him (Bible reading), when we no longer practice assembling ourselves together with the family of God (church attendance), and when we discontinue our service to the Lord (serving others).

We no longer experience gladness in the Lord when we lose that longing and yearning to seek to know more about Him. If the desire to nurture what we have with God is no longer present, we will experience dissatisfaction and discontentment in our walk with Him. The good thing to know is that it need not stay that way! Putting forth effort to spend time with God in prayer, Bible reading, church involvement, and in serving others will bring "freshness" to our walk and a spark of fire in our relationship with Him (and others).

The faithful love of the Lord never ends! His mercies never cease. Great is his faithfulness; his mercies begin afresh each morning.

Lamentations 3:22, 23 (NLT)

For he satisfies the thirsty and fills the hungry with good things.

Psalm 107:9 (NLT)

...my people shall be satisfied with my goodness, saith the Lord.

Jeremiah 31:14 (KJV)

Promises

Ralph will not make a promise. He takes this very seriously. I do not believe he has ever promised me anything (excluding our wedding vows). I tried to get him to promise me something when we were dating and he refused. He let me know that I would probably not get many promises out of him, if any. His word is to be taken as said and he will do the best he can in keeping it. Otherwise, he goes no further in pledging something he may not be able to keep.

Ralph believes in his words being kept to a minimum …hence, a short story.

The Bible says for us to not be hasty in what we are about to say. We are to be careful with making promises and breaking those promises, especially to God. It would be better to not make a promise than to have to break it. That's why the Word says to let our words be few in number.

People should be able to count on what we tell them. Granted, there are times when things happen beyond our control and we cannot keep our word. That is to be understood, but always contact that person and explain what happened. It will not take long before you are dubbed "not dependable" when continuous engagements or appointments are broken and you never offer an explanation.

Before our day ever begins, we should seek God in what we should say. Pray that the words you speak are words of "life and not death." That is just a way of saying, be positive and not negative. Keep your word. We should not be hasty to speak when we should keep quiet (and we generally are aware of this). Our words are quite powerful.

> Be not rash with thy mouth, and let not thine heart be hasty to utter *any* thing before God: for God is in heaven, and thou upon earth: therefore let thy words be few.

> Ecclesiastes 5:2 (KJV)

When you make a promise to God, don't delay in following through, for God takes no pleasure in fools. Keep all the promises you make to him. It is better to say nothing than to make a promise and not keep it.

Ecclesiastes 5:4, 5 (NLT)

...You must not break your vows; you must carry out the vows you make to the Lord.

Matthew 5:33 (NLT)

...he that refraineth his lips is wise.

Proverbs 10:19 (KJV).

...Be sensible and keep your mouth shut.

(NLT version of same verse)

To Be Loved

Ralph is a loving man—one who is not afraid to show love, emotion and sensitivity. Not only do I benefit from this man's love and affection, but our sons greatly benefit from their father who loves them dearly.

Ralph is very quick to give an embrace whenever I or the boys need to feel his arms around us. He is a man, you know, what we come to expect a man to be: macho, athletic (used to be), strong, etc. Ralph is all those things, yet a loving man and father.

Our boys will be able to express love to their spouses and their own children someday because of the example set by their father. It is so important to understand that our children will treat their own spouses and kids much the same way they see their parents treat each other and themselves while growing up.

A loving father; that is what stands out about Ralph. Every disciplined measure for the boys is motivated out of love. He has reiterated many times over to our boys that no matter what mistakes they make they will still be loved. What a wonderful thing to know! To be loved even though we mess up or fail at something that was important. That kind of love really binds a family together through the tough times, as well as the good.

Our heavenly Father is *love*. He loves you and me in the here and now. He truly exhibits an unconditional love that we, His children, are still working on. The greatest proof of that love came when God sent His only Son to die on a cross so you and I could come to know Him as Lord of our lives.

I believe Jesus is less harsh on us than we are on ourselves or with each other. He is not one to cast aside or withhold His love because we disappoint Him or mess up. How many times has He given us second chances?

Nothing can separate us from the love of God. He is consistent in His love towards His children and He loves all mankind. God truly wants *all* to know Him. He extends an invitation to "whosoever will."

It is up to you and me to accept His love by acknowledging Jesus' death on the cross and saying "yes" to Him in our lives. Let Him be that loving Father to you.

> For God so loved the world, that he gave his only begotten Son, that whosoever believeth in him should not perish, but have everlasting life.

John 3:16 (KJV)

> All that the Father giveth me shall come to me; and him that cometh to me I will in no wise cast out.

John 6:37 (KJV)

> ...for God is love.

I John 4:8 (KJV)

Wait, Please

Some decisions in life will have to be made "on the spot." Others can afford a little time, and it probably is wise to take all the time allotted before we make such decisions.

I am guilty of being hasty in making decisions that really should not have been made until all angles had been thoroughly examined. Ralph has to step in (too often) and gently nudge me to slow down, remind me that we do not have to make a decision right now, and to take the time we do have to think on it a bit. I am impulsive in areas such as buying a new car, furniture or clothes, you know, all those things that can't possibly wait another day before making a decision on purchasing them.

Ralph says that the car will still be there tomorrow, regardless of what the salesman implies. He insists on shopping around before purchasing certain items. I like to get the first thing I see—just the idea of getting it, buying it and having it now! And, oh yes, most of the time I find a better selection later.

I'm thinking, *Ralph, how can you be so patient, so slow, so unhurried to make some decisions?* I'm really glad he has brought balance to this marriage in the area of decision making. He has allowed me to have "my way" a few times and, yeah, "we" regretted the decision "I" made. *By the way, I wish I had listened to you about our living room suit ... the one that didn't last long ... remember? Oh well, next time I won't be so hasty (maybe) to make a decision and will take advantage of time (especially when there is no time limit). I do know (now) that you are not just trying to be mean or difficult when you say, "Let's wait ... look around a bit." Oh, you are so wise! (I'm growing wiser myself. Did you say something, dear?).*

Waiting on the Lord can be frustrating! Many times we feel because we have to wait that He is not working in our behalf. Being consumed with "when" is costly to our peace of mind. Jesus reminds us many times to wait on Him and He will strengthen us. It may be that we feel He isn't working fast enough, so we decide to get the ball rolling and pry windows and doors open that are not yet meant to be opened.

Acknowledging Him in everything we do is necessary. He will be with us in making those decisions—those that have to be made "on the spot" and those that don't. Take advantage of time when it is on your side and allow God to help you in making a wise choice that will be best for all concerned. Most of our choices affect others.

Being hasty in our actions can cause serious problems in our relationships. Sometimes the best course of action is none at all until time has been spent with God in prayer on the subject matter. We can only see what lies clearly at hand. God knows the next turn, the next hill, and the next road ahead. Isn't it about time you found out His perspective on the matter at hand before making your decision?

> Wait on the Lord: be of good courage, and he shall strengthen thine heart: wait, I say, on the Lord.

Psalm 27:14 (KJV)

> I waited patiently for the Lord to help me, and he turned to me and heard my cry.

Psalm 40:1 (NLT)

In all thy ways acknowledge Him, and he shall direct thy paths.

Proverbs 3:6 (KJV)

Trust Me

"Trust me" ... those two words are rarely spoken between Ralph and myself, yet they are there as sure as our love for each other. I know Ralph well enough that whenever we face a difficult situation that trust is there. Many times I am not sure about a change that comes in our lives and how it will affect us. It is really good to know that when I look into my husband's eyes, trust is conveyed without it ever being spoken.

I fell in love with this man and I don't have to wonder if he is coming home at the end of the day. He loves me and our boys more than anything else. I know he will do what he can to ensure our safety, welfare, and happiness.

There have been times (and more will follow) when our lives changed drastically, and I looked to him for *some* kind of confirmation that everything would be okay. He has done "*real fine*" in this area. He is there in his own special way. He makes things easier by just being himself …the loving and trustworthy man he is.

It is great to know that in all of life's ups and downs, I have a partner who makes it very easy to believe that everything will be okay …as long as we have God and each other.

Our being able to trust each other stems from God in our lives. He truly is the One that we have put our whole trust in. God knows exactly what I need to get through tough times and I have learned to trust Him (and will continue to do so).

The old song "Tis So Sweet to Trust in Jesus" is a lived experience for me. Over the years, I have come to rely on the Lord and He has never failed me. Oh yes, many times life is hard and I can't say it's "all fun," but He has taught me to trust Him daily. He is my deliverer—my strength and comfort when things cannot be fixed or altered. Often, He changes me instead of the circumstances, and I find His faithfulness to be true as I trust Him.

Lord, I am so glad I have You to lean on and to run to when things get overwhelming. You truly are my hiding place, and I know that You work all things out for my good.

Blessed is the man that maketh the Lord his trust ...

Psalm 40:4 (KJV)

My goodness, and my fortress; my high tower, and my deliverer; my shield, and he in whom I trust ...

Psalm 144:2 (KJV)

For thou art my hope, O Lord God: thou art my trust from my youth.

Psalm 71:5 (KJV)

Contentment

It is a Saturday night around 9:00. I am watching TV with Ralph. He sits in his big lounge chair and I in my rocker. We are both reading. I leave the room and write what is my last devotional in this book.

I completely feel content with my life. I am absolutely fulfilled as a wife, mother and child of God. Do I have problems? Oh yeah, and some are quite large. Do I have everything I desire? No, but I have what I need. There is this definite feeling and knowing in my heart that I am *satisfied* with my life. I feel blessed to be able to say that.

Ralph, you, along with God, is the reason I can make this statement of contentment. We will always be okay as long as we keep God first in our lives, and each other first in our thoughts, actions, care, and commitment in our marriage. I love you!

Brandon and Zach, the treasure of our lives, we pray you find the kind of love we share. You will. God has already picked out the ladies you are meant to share your lives with. He knows them by name. We take comfort in this. Part of our contentment is knowing we have done our best in raising you guys. We see you exceeding above what we hoped you might be. We love you!

Readers, my desires are that you will take these devotions and allow God to speak to your heart. Hopefully, you will see how blessed you are. Perhaps, you have learned something through what God has given me. Apply what His Word has spoken in these devotions. In doing this, I believe you will experience contentment in your own marriage and life.

God, you are contentment. You bring that blessed peace and restfulness to our souls. Thank you, that we can be satisfied in such a discontented world. That only comes in accepting you as Savior of our lives. I made that choice (soon-to-be) forty-four years ago … and I have never regretted that decision. I love You! Thanks for loving me!

Yet true godliness with contentment is itself great wealth.

I Timothy 6:6 (NLT)

So if we have enough food and clothing, let us be content.

I Timothy 6:8 (NLT)

...I have learned, in whatsoever state I am, *therewith* to be content.

Philippians 4:11 (KJV)

...*and be* content with such things as ye have: for he hath said, I will never leave thee, nor forsake thee.

Hebrews 13:5 (KJV)